EYES ON MIME

Marcel Marceau leaning on an invisible mantelpiece.

EYES ON MIME

Language Without Speech

KATHRINE SORLEY WALKER

The John Day Company   New York

Library of Congress Catalogue Card Number: 69-10809

PRINTED IN THE UNITED STATES OF AMERICA

ACKNOWLEDGMENTS

For permission to use photographs on the pages shown thanks are due to Anthony Crickmay (frontispiece, 105, 114, 117, 141, 148, 150, 154); Houston Rogers (16); Paul Hansen (26); Australian News & Info. Bureau (43); Marilyn Silverstone (53); Japan Info. Center, London (57, 59); Marc Alexander (62); Thailand Info. Service, London (66); Friedman-Abeles (70); Raymond Mander & Joe Mitchenson (73, 80); Société Nouvelle Pathé Cinéma (78); Soviet News Agency, London (84); Felix Fonteyn (86); Central News Agency, Taipei (88); Enthoven Coll. London (94, 97, 98, 103); James Howell (109); G. Proano-Moreno (112); Zoe Dominic (145); National Theater of the Deaf (167).

Contents

INTRODUCTION   11

Part I: THE CHARACTER OF MIME   13

Part II: THE CHRONOLOGY OF MIME   42

Part III: AN EXCURSION INTO TECHNIQUE   120

Part IV: MIME IN DAILY LIFE   158

Part V: PATHS AHEAD   170

SELECTED BIBLIOGRAPHY   180

SELECTED FILMOGRAPHY   182

INDEX   185

ILLUSTRATIONS

Marcel Marceau leaning on an invisible
mantelpiece   Frontispiece

Margot Fonteyn in *Giselle* (Royal Ballet)   16

Lucia Chase and Royes Fernandez in *Swan Lake*
(American Ballet Theater)   26

Charlie Chaplin in *The Gold Rush*   39

Australian corroboree   43

Balasaraswathi (Bharata-nātya, India)   53

Nō theater, Japan   57

Tsuchigumo—"The Spider" (Azuma Kabuki, Japan)   59

Kathakali company of Kerala Kalamandalam, India,
in *Rāmāyana*   62

Traditional dance drama, Thailand   66

The dumb show from John Gielgud's modern dress
production of *Hamlet*   70

John Rich as Harlequin   73

Les Enfants du Paradis (Jean-Louis Barrault as
Deburau)   78

Joseph Grimaldi as Clown   80

Circus clown, United States—Emmett Kelly   82

Circus clown, U.S.S.R.—Oleg Popov   84

Pantomimeteater, Tivoli, Copenhagen, Denmark   86

The Monkey God (Peking Opera)   88

Fred Farren as Dr. Coppélius in *Coppélia*, England,
1906   94

Illustrations

Adeline Genée as Swanilda and Dorothy Craske as Franz in *Coppélia,* England, 1906   94

Jane May in *L'Enfant Prodigue,* 1891   97

Jane May and Francesca Zanfretta in *L'Enfant Prodigue,* 1891   98

Tamara Karsavina as Columbine in *Carnaval*   103

Marcel Marceau playing the violin   105

Jacques Tati in *Jour de Fête*   107

City Center Joffrey Ballet in *The Green Table*   109

Charles Weidman in *Pantomime* from *Suite Intriga*   112

Martha Graham in *Clytemnestra*   114

The Forest (African Ballet of Guinea)   117

Edward Villella in *Prodigal Son* (New York City Ballet)   141

Margot Fonteyn in *Romeo and Juliet* (Royal Ballet)   145

Nadia Nerina and Stanley Holden in *La Fille mal Gardée* (Royal Ballet)   148

Robert Helpmann and Frederick Ashton in *Cinderella* (Royal Ballet)   150

Alexander Grant, Stanley Holden, and Leslie Edwards in *La Fille mal Gardée* (Royal Ballet)   154

National Theater of the Deaf in *Gianni Schicchi*   167

Adam Darius   174

Ladislav Fialka group, Prague, in *The Fools*   176

Ladislav Fialka group, Prague, in *The Road*   178

INTRODUCTION

Everyone in the world uses mime, although it is rarely given the name. When people are too far away for voices to be heard, they beckon, they signal, they communicate by gestures of all kinds. When they have no common language, in a foreign country, they mime what they need—they raise imaginary cups to drink from; they pretend to sleep or wash their hands or eat. And sometimes, when words are difficult to find, when emotion is great, gesture takes over—an arm goes around someone's shoulders or a hand on a head. Mime, then, is more natural than one's native language—indeed, a child mimes before he speaks.

Natural abilities, however, are merely raw material. To be able to speak or sing in the way most people can or run or dance never means that one can speak poetry, sing grand opera, break athletic records, or star in ballet. All these feats require special gifts, specially and vigorously trained, and the kinds of gestures we all make to help us along in life are very much merely the raw material of the art of mime.

Origins are always hard to trace. Most things, instead of beginning on one special date, gradually evolve. All art forms did this. Painting built up slowly from rough marks on the ground or on the walls of caves; drama and literature from the early storyteller gathering an audience around a camp-fire; dance and ballet from the instinctive rhythmic movement of primitive peoples.

Mime has similar origins to both drama and the dance. When the storyteller was lost for words, gesture took over.

His description of an animal hunt, for instance, was filled out by action—he showed which beast had been stalked, and how; how the hunter had flung his weapon; and if the man had been killed, how the animal had turned on him. Words never seemed to him explicit enough or dramatic enough—he wanted to make his audience *see* exactly what had happened. The desire continues in primitive communities all over the world.

As an art, however, mime has had many branches. Taken as the accomplishment of conveying sense without speech, by imitating action, or by using gestures which someone else understands, it plays an important part in all the dramatic arts.

Each branch has its own idiom. The mime used in classical ballet is unlike that in plays; silent film mime or circus clown mime is different from the technique of the pantomime theaters of France or Denmark; other schools of dance, in particular those of India, China, and Japan, have specialized gesture languages of their own. There are points where they overlap, but they each have an individual character; all require training to be performed and some call for special knowledge to be understood.

All, however, are rewarding. In straight plays, the actor who can mime adds another dimension to his acting; in opera, particularly comic opera, the singer who can mime is an invaluable asset; no ballerina can reach the heights of *Giselle* or *Swan Lake* unless she is expert in the art, and all narrative ballets, old and new, in Western or Eastern style, employ their native gesture language to tell their stories. It is remarkable and fascinating just how clearly and fully one can come to understand what is never put into words.

Part I

THE CHARACTER OF MIME

Before we go back in time to the origins of mime, let's take a look at the present. What kind of mime can we see today?

For most people the immediate link is through the classical ballet, and in ballet there are really two distinct meanings of the word. There is the traditional gesture language of the classical dance technique, and there is silent acting.

All the famous nineteenth-century ballets, *Swan Lake* or *Giselle* or *The Sleeping Beauty,* tell their stories in gesture language. In those days mime and dance remained separate in the structure of a ballet, as *Giselle,* for instance, shows very clearly.

It opens with a mimed scene. Albrecht tells us that he is wearing his plain peasant's costume because he is in love with a beautiful girl who lives in the cottage we can see on the left-hand side of the stage. His squire, Wilfred, remonstrates with him in vain and then reminds him that he is still wearing his sword which will show he is a nobleman. Albrecht takes it off, gives it to him, and waves him away.

How is this conveyed to us without words? Albrecht indicates himself in the universal way, pointing to himself with his right forefinger. The gesture that means the way he is dressed is a sweeping one, with both hands, inward and then outward, from shoulder to hip. Then there follows the "me" gesture again; then the hands upturned and crossed at the wrists in front of the heart, which means love; the right hand, with the thumb next to the face, describing a circle around the face from right to left, which means beautiful; and the pointing finger again, this time toward the cottage on our left. Wilfred pleads with him with arms forward and hands upturned. Albrecht shakes his head and moves his hands, turned downward, across each other in a negative gesture. Wilfred points to the sword. Albrecht takes it off, hands it to him, and, with his right arm outstretched, gestures dismissal.

Now some of these gestures are in everyday use—head-shaking, pointing, and so on. Others are purely identified with classical ballet—the love gesture or the movement that means beautiful (really, a beautiful person). These, with others, crop up in ballet after ballet, and as we learn their meanings, we find we are understanding shades of significance that passed us by before. We begin to realize that if we know what these gestures mean, a really expert mime using them can make it almost unnecessary for us to have a printed synopsis of a ballet's story.

Giselle is a good example of this. All we need to know is in fact conveyed by gestures during the course of the ballet. Sometimes it is so clear that mentally one hears words. Albrecht holds out his arms to Giselle, touches his lips with his right forefinger; she shakes her head; he raises the forefinger; she laughingly kisses hers and presses it to his lips. "Give me a kiss," one almost hears. "No . . ." "Just one!" And she compromises. . . .

The hunting party of the Duke of Courland and his daughter Bathilde arrives, and when Giselle's mother, Berthe, comes out of her cottage, the squire asks her if she will bring out a table and something to drink. "Bring" is a gesture of sweeping both arms, hands upturned, from right to left—if the cottage were on his left, of course, he would reverse that. For a table, his hands, palms downward, are crossed in front and then moved apart to each side, indicating a large, flat surface. For a drink, he pours from an invisible jug with his right hand and then raises the hand, fist clenched but thumb pointing to his mouth, and tips his head slightly back. The next moment we see it all happen. The mother nods her head in understanding, bobs a curtsy, gestures to the young village people to carry out the instructions. They go into the cottage for a table and beakers, while Giselle brings the jug of wine.

These gestures join those for love and a beautiful person as part of our classical ballet vocabulary, and the conversation shortly afterward between Giselle and Princess Bathilde enlarges it further. Giselle bends down, unseen by Bathilde, to stroke the rich material of her skirt and lay her cheek on it. Bathilde feels the slight pull on her dress and rises. She looks at her father and gestures that Giselle is beautiful (the right hand circling the face, as Albrecht did earlier) and then asks Giselle (hands upturned in inquiry) about herself. Giselle makes an odd gesture of holding something in the air with her left hand and a plucking movement downward with her right. There are alternative explanations of the meaning of this—one is that it represents the plucking of grapes from the vine; another that it signifies carding and spinning. Perhaps the latter is more probable—usually grapes are cut by the bunch, carefully, and not stripped from the branches. Bathilde asks whether she likes doing this work, and Giselle answers that she prefers dancing.

The gesture for dancing is arms raised high above the head and hands circling each other. Actually we have seen

15

Margot Fonteyn in *Giselle* (Royal Ballet)

it before in *Giselle* and can see it in every other traditional ballet whenever someone suggests a dance or announces a dance. Giselle then dances a few steps around Bathilde. Her mother realizes what she is doing and, as she has told us earlier, in a scene we will go into in a moment, tells Bathilde in horror that if Giselle dances, she will die—hands twirling over her head for dancing, then plunging, crossed, downward in the violently final gesture which means death. Bathilde, trying to think of some way in which to comfort Giselle, turns to her father, asks his permission to give Giselle the necklace she is wearing (the "me" gesture, and touching the necklace with a look of inquiry), takes it off, and puts it over Giselle's head, telling her it was a present from her fiancé (the "me" gesture and pointing at the third finger of her left hand with her right forefinger). This is an ambiguous gesture that is used for betrothal but can mean marriage. You will notice, in *Swan Lake,* when Von Rothbart asks Siegfried in the ballroom scene to swear he will marry Odile, he uses this gesture. (For swearing he raises the first two fingers on the right hand, turned outward, with the arm up.)

Giselle's mother has told us earlier why she is so distressed about Giselle's love of dancing. This is sometimes given in its full version, sometimes it is very much cut, but if it is well done, it is interesting to watch. She says that if Giselle dances too much, she will kill herself, and then she will join the Wilis, who are spirits, with wreaths on their heads and tiny wings, who rise from their graves and dance in the woods at night. They make any man who meets them dance until he drops down dead.

This scene starts with the dance gesture and then the death gesture, when Berthe speaks to Bathilde. Then Berthe raises her hands, turned toward her face, arms bent at the elbow—this indicates a body in a grave; she bends down,

then, as she rises, sweeps both arms upward and sideways—
to show the spirits coming from the graves. This, as you will
realize if you try it, is actually the same gesture the squire
used for "bring out," only angled differently, so that "bring
out" turns into "rise up." She indicates a wreath on her head;
then she puts her hands back to back behind her at the
waist, where they immediately look like the little butterfly
wings that romantic spirits in ballet, like Wilis or sylphids,
usually wear. Then once again come the gestures for dancing and dying.

Now this is not quite so clear as simple question and answer. Usually narrative mime has to be slightly pieced out
with program explanation. From what Berthe tells us, all we
would discover is that if Giselle dances, she will die, and that
this is connected with dead bodies in graves whose spirits
rise up, wearing wreaths and wings, and that there is more
dancing and dying after that. She does not tell us that the
spirits not only dance themselves, but also entice men to
dance with them until they drop down dead.

All the same, because of the way she uses these gestures,
we know at least that there is great menace in these dancing
spirits, and the basic gestures of classical mime are, of course,
always amplified by the talented dancer, through bearing
and facial expression.

When the tragedy of *Giselle* comes to its climax at the
end of Act I, and Giselle goes mad and dies, some of the
gestures we have described are used again. The duke and
Bathilde, coming from the cottage, ask Albrecht why he is
wearing his peasant's clothes; it is the same gesture with
which he opened the ballet. When Giselle, rushing between
Albrecht and Bathilde, points to her ring finger to say he is
her fiancé, Bathilde counters with the same movement.

Act II is almost all dancing, although it begins with mime.

The Character of Mime

The Queen of the Wilis conjures up her subjects, and this time the rise up gesture is slightly altered—it has many variations. With her hands at her sides, she makes a gesture as if she were scooping up individual weights on right and left at the same moment, implying that the Wilis will rise from their graves. They appear, of course, from each side, mysteriously veiled—no theater has enough trapdoors to bring them all from under the stage! The queen wears no veil, but she moves her hands and arms as if she were lifting and throwing off a veil, and the Wilis imitate her, *actually* lifting their veils and moving offstage briefly to throw them aside. After some dancing they gather round Giselle's grave as her spirit materializes and joins them. Then, hearing Albrecht approach, they vanish.

The presence of the grave cross onstage, often bearing the name Giselle, makes it easy for Albrecht to explain that he is mourning for Giselle. He indicates "me," points to the cross, and then, with the fingers of both hands, traces on his face the marks of tears running down his cheeks. This is the sorrow gesture. Wilfred, calling Albrecht's attention by touching his shoulder as he kneels by the cross, begs him (the gesture of hands clasped and raised with the arms bent at the elbows) to come away—once more the gesture that means removal from one place to another, that in Act I said "bring out" or "rise up." Albrecht shakes his head, gestures no, and dismisses him.

Then Giselle's spirit appears to Albrecht. They dance, but when she leaves him temporarily, he tells us, in a series of very beautiful movements, that she is gone—the spirit (a sweeping up-and-down arm gesture which indicates flight) he loves (the love gesture) comes (bringing gestures from each side alternately) not (the no gesture). All these movements are linked so that they are like a snatch of dancing, but they are in fact mime. Mime, when it is properly done by the dancer, when one gesture moves into another, as one phrase moves into another in a spoken sentence, and links perfectly with the musical accompaniment and is given with the body as well as the hands and arms, becomes a part of dancing. You can see how it is possible just to stand stock-still, face expressionless, and make some gesture—the sorrow gesture, for instance, with your fingers moving down your cheeks as if they were following falling tears. Try it, looking in a mirror; then try it, letting your shoulders relax forward, your head incline slightly to one side, your expression become sad—and see how much more it means.

The next tiny mime scene in *Giselle* comes when Albrecht is caught by the Wilis and comes rushing on to beg for his life. He kneels to the queen and clasps his hands in the gesture with which Wilfred, earlier, begged him to leave the grave. The queen points to him and then repeats the gesture Giselle's mother used in Act I for dancing and dying.

How variously the dance gesture can be used! Giselle, in her happiness at the beginning of the ballet, twisted her hands gaily above her head as she asked Albrecht to dance with her. How different that was from Myrtha's imperious commanding movement now, as, time and again, she orders her victim to dance. The manner in which a gesture is used is like the tone of voice in which a word is said—it clarifies and amplifies the meaning.

Giselle, however, as well as being a typical early-nine-teenth-century ballet (it was first danced in 1841), using classical mime to tell its story, is a ballet with important acting parts, so that it also illustrates the other branch of mime, silent acting. Every classical dancer knows, to a greater or lesser extent, the vocabulary of gesture and how to use all these significant movements of head and arm and hand and, by using them, to ask and answer questions or give some simple description. Through this silent language they can tell us facts about the story and the action, but *feeling* and *character* need much more than gesture to convey them.

Take, for instance, the classic gesture for love—a beautiful one, even at its most formal, the position indicating that the heart is involved, the crossed wrists and slightly curled hands suggesting tenderness and care. But how different it can look when real warmth of feeling lies behind the gesture from when it is done as an exercise by students at rehearsal! Implying real feeling not only involves the hands and arms, but also shows in the facial expression, the light in the eyes, the angle of the head and of the shoulders, and we realize, seeing this difference, that this is basically what acting in ballet is about. It is the art of expressing every shade of feeling clearly to an audience and utilizing every physical means to do so.

The great mime uses, in turn or all together, every nerve and muscle in his body, but that is not all, because acting cannot be purely physical. The essence of his art is that each nerve and muscle are employed as servant of his heart and mind, to express the feelings of the character he is portraying.

Classical ballet has never laid down as clearly as have, for instance, the schools of dance in India, the basic feelings that a mime must know how to express. There a student is taught nine sentiments with their accompanying moods. Sometimes a dancer will give a demonstration of these which is quite fascinating. By carefully worked-out combinations of facial expression, using the eye and eyebrow muscles to a much greater extent than most Western dance does and hand and arm movements (and these dancers have extraordinarily flexible hands and fingers), he conveys in sequence love, anger, courage, amusement, compassion, aversion, amazement, fear, and peace. For love, he has drooping eyelids and side glances; for anger, wide-open eyes with dilated pupils and grinding teeth; for courage, a lofty glance and flung-back head; for amusement, arched eyebrows and a slightly tossing head; for compassion—a variant on love—tender sidelong looks; for aversion, contracted eyes and pouting lips; for amazement (which is basically *amused amazement*), a variation on the theme of arched eyebrows and incredulous smile; for fear, dilated nostrils and eyes rolling from side to side; for peace, a look of contemplation, with closed eyes or an upturned glance.

Classical ballet achieves its own versions of each of these moods. Frequently they are a combination of some classical gesture with the dancer's own strength of expression, as we have seen with the love gesture. They are much more individually flexible and diverse in character, much less formally laid down, than their Indian equivalents, and our dancers cannot employ such meticulously worked-out movements of eyes, eyebrows, or lips. They vary more from one artist to another and are so much part of the character study or the interpretation of the story that they are rarely thought of as mime or gesture. They arise naturally out of the action and seem a part of it.

Giselle gives opportunities for many of these expressions. Basically a dramatic ballet, its leading roles are challenges to ballerina and *premier danseur*.

In the course of the action, Giselle must express gaiety, shyness, love, annoyance (with Hilarion), admiration (over Bathilde), doubt, dismay, and various stages of mental disturbance—among other shades of emotion. Albrecht must be authoritative, tender, gay, taken aback (at sight of Bathilde and her father), distressed, angry, and grief-stricken. Frequently the movements laid down by the choreography, either for dance or gesture, convey these moods, but they go for very little unless the dancers augment them by feeling and expression.

In addition to the two leading roles in *Giselle*, there are five subsidiary roles which can show the ability of classical mimes. Each of these must be considered and studied by the dancer so that the character is projected to us, in the audience, and thoughts and reactions are made clear and vital. Of course, it very rarely happens that all five are in the hands of equally able actor-dancers!

The first thing we realize, probably, when we think about the minor roles is that just as much as the major, they are open to different interpretations. It is surprising perhaps that so frequently different dancers make them look like carbon copies of one another. In fact, there can be a variety of styles. Hilarion, for instance, can be played as a villain, forcing his attentions on Giselle against her will and taking his revenge on Albrecht as soon as he can. It is equally legitimate, however, to play him as a previously favored suitor, now hurt and wronged and, above all, certain that Giselle is being betrayed by her new lover. Between these two are quite a few possible permutations. The mother is rarely played differently—she is always very elderly, anxious, prophesying woe, and getting it. It would be interesting to see a younger and jollier conception. Bathilde is frequently merely a nonentity, but she can be more; always a great lady confronted with a difficult situation, she can be genuinely kind or merely patronizing to Giselle, touched in her love or only in her pride by Albrecht's conduct. Wilfred the squire and the Duke of Courland are much less important, but they can be played intelligently and individually.

In other words, all these five must do certain things; they must "speak" certain phrases of gesture language. But they can work out a character for themselves, as actors would, that fits the action, and then, by facial expression, by the way they use the gestures and the thought behind them, by the makeup they decide on, they can convey their individual interpretation of the part to us.

Giselle ends with the saving of Albrecht's life through Giselle's encouragement and love; every time he almost gives up dancing through weariness, she urges him on, and at last the dawn breaks and the power of the Wilis deserts them for the daylight hours. But this is not really told in mime; it is conveyed to us by the other expressive elements of a ballet: the dancing, the action, the music—all showing the increasing desperation and then the feeling of relief—and the stage lighting, which suggests the light of day.

The vocabulary of classical ballet gesture that *Giselle* has yielded will help us understand a great deal of the mime in other traditional ballets. In fact, once you know some of these basic word-signs, you find them again and again, in different contexts. It is like learning a few really useful words of some foreign language with which you can get around the country with added ease. Take *Swan Lake*—although there are so many different productions of *Swan Lake* nowadays that one cannot be certain any particular mime scene will be included. All the same, it is possible that when you see a Swan Queen, she will tell Siegfried (and, incidentally, us) that the lake was made from her mother's tears. For the lake, she turns toward the back of the stage and, bending slightly, repeats the gesture that the squire in *Gi-*

selle used at a higher level to indicate a table—crossing her hands in front of her and then moving them apart to each side, as if they were sliding along a large, flat surface. There is, of course, probably a lake painted on the backdrop, so that her gesture becomes plainer than it would be in a rehearsal room. Then she turns, crosses her arms across her breast, not in the love gesture over the heart but in a centralized position—this means mother. Then she strokes her cheeks in the sorrow or tears gesture.

Again, if you see *Swan Lake* in its entirety, you will probably at some point see the drinking gestures used, when Siegfried is drinking with his friends. You will see the Princess Mother indicate that Siegfried should dance with his guests in the ballroom scene. The flight gesture that Albrecht used for Giselle's spirit comes into use to show the flight of birds—of swans, in fact. And you will notice that some basic gesture of this sort reveals which of its meanings is in question by the context of the scene. Just as the flight gesture would hardly mean birds or swans in *Giselle* and does mean a flying spirit, so it obviously means swans, rather than spirits, in the connection of *Swan Lake.*

A new gesture turns up in *Swan Lake* when Siegfried talks about going swan shooting. He extends his left arm upward, as if he were holding an invisible crossbow and with the right hand makes a pulling movement toward himself as if drawing back the bolt of the crossbow. This is used throughout *Swan Lake* but not elsewhere—it comes into the category of a gesture which indicates some specialized action.

How often you see children in play grab an invisible gun out of its holster, aim, and shoot at the enemy! The crossbow shooting gesture is exactly the same; it simulates the action and so would be clear to anyone who knew how the weapon is handled. You can fight with invisible swords or

25

Lucia Chase and Royes Fernandez in *Swan Lake* (American Ballet Theater)

daggers (although they often use stage props, as in the fights in *Romeo and Juliet*); you can fling invisible stones or strangle someone with an invisible scarf. If you want to indicate that it *is* a scarf, untie it at your neck, take it off, move it as if you were holding it by its end—and the audience will see a scarf.

Working gestures are like fighting ones—descriptive of action. Watch for them. It may be a harvest scene (as in *La Fille mal Gardée*), when the peasants use stage-prop scythes with the appropriate sort of movement. It may be sewing (the stepsisters do this in Ashton's *Cinderella*), sweeping (Cinderella does this herself), milking cows, or driving horses.

Gestures like these are the offspring of the child's game of make-believe, when he drives cars or flies like an airplane or rides a pony. The essentials are that the gesture should express as clearly as possible the action it relates to. But you will find, at various points, that a basic gesture can be in some way modified when used in a ballet. Think of speech—how, instead of "should not," we say (and nowadays even write) "shouldn't," how we use some familiar short phrase which really means a much longer one. This happens in movement, especially when it is incorporated into the dance, but you will find it fairly easy to link the more academic phrase with the colloquial. It will be something like the no gesture, which, instead of being made by both hands in front of the dancer, can be made by one hand only and in a great many positions.

Working gestures appear in most dance traditions. In India they dance an excerpt from a story about the god Krishna, which shows milking and churning, and because these are basically done in the same way, they are clear to Western audiences. A Chinese dance excerpt is about an old boatman who punts his boat to a landing stage, takes on a woman passenger, and resumes the journey. His movements of punting, tying up the boat (staggering slightly as it washes against the bank), helping her in, taking up the pole, and gradually getting into the smoother rhythm again are universal. This is not gesture language, but it *is* mime, for it conveys the description of a happening. Its charm lies in the fact that every moment is make-believe, yet every movement is so well observed and so naturally made that a complete picture comes into the minds of an audience.

It is this type of mime that is characteristic of the repertoire of the French pantomime artists, the best known of whom is probably Marcel Marceau. Some of his most popular and enjoyable pieces are in exactly this category. They are make-believe accounts of ordinary everyday events. At one time he will be a billposter, carrying bucket and brush, ladder and roll of bills, running up and down the ladder, slapping on the bills, taking time off to watch what is going on in the street. At another he will evoke people and actions that anyone can watch in a public park. All this is an extension of the Guess What I'm Doing game we all play as children or the charades that were so popular as a party game once upon a time, when two parts of a word, say, "shoeshine," and then the whole word were acted in little scenes without speech: first, someone trying on a shoe (only one—that was important); then someone polishing a piece of silver so that it would shine brightly; and then someone rubbing up another's shoes. The difference (apart from standard of performance) is that the charade allowed props to be used, but in the pantomime scene everything is imaginary. Some actions, of course, can never be made intelligible. I remember one music hall actor doing a skit to this effect—

standing perfectly still with his eyes turned up or perfectly still with his eyes turned down—the explanation being that he was going up or down in an elevator.

As well as working scenes and fighting scenes, there are sports and games scenes in ballet, and have been ever since Roman mimes acted out make-believe wrestling matches to popular acclaim. Every action in everyday life can be imitated, and so it can become part of the gesture language of the dance. But sports are primarily movement, after all, as is dance itself, so that they become less and less mime or gesture. Any ball game, if it were represented in dance, would be done by reproducing its actual movements, cut or modified for the stage, but only if, for instance, some altercation between players and referee were in question, would mime be called into play—for a protest, a refusal, or a reaction or feeling of some sort.

Now, in traditional ballets, as once in the straight theater, there were careful divisions between tragedy and comedy, and in dancing we find that the mime in a comedy ballet, such as *Coppélia,* is slightly different, or at least done differently, from that of the other nineteenth-century ballets we see.

Coppélia is, first and foremost, a comedy romance. It is about a pair of village lovers, Swanilda and Franz, and sometimes the mime is woven into the dancing. Right at the beginning, Swanilda is alone on stage except for the doll Coppélia, who sits, apparently absorbed in a book, in the window of the toymaker Coppélius' house. Swanilda begins her dance by beckoning with her left hand to Coppélia, an invitation to come down and talk to her. When there is no response, she shakes both fists to show her displeasure, pirouettes away, and ends, looking to her right, away from Coppélia, but with her arms extended to the left, hands turned up, palms out, in the gesture of refusal or rejection.

Now this dance has an important difference from the variation Swanilda will dance in the last act, which is really a divertissement of dances. It actually says something—it incorporates these snatches of gesture language because it is continuing the story. When it ends, we have progressed with the ballet's narrative, not just watched an attractive piece of dancing. We have learned that Swanilda has asked Coppélia, who she thinks is a real girl, to come join her and is annoyed because she seems superior and unfriendly.

Once Swanilda has gone off crossly, Franz enters. He knocks at her cottage door, gets no reply, shrugs his shoulders, notices Coppélia in the window, tells us that she is beautiful, bows to her, and throws kisses. Of course, no response. While he is doing this, Swanilda returns. She is pleased to see him, straightens her dress and cap, tiptoes up to him, and waits for him to see her. When his attention is still elsewhere, she looks around, sees what he is doing (and by this time old Coppélius has mischievously got behind Coppélia and is manipulating her arm so that she is throwing kisses back to Franz), and is outraged. She then pretends she doesn't really care and goes off without Franz's noticing her at all. All this is conveyed, not mainly by conventional gesture, but by facial expression.

How often, when one is trying to describe somebody who is very fascinating and animated, one says, "Well, she's not exactly pretty, but she has a very expressive face." Some people *are* like that—across their faces all kinds of expressions move, sometimes in such rapid succession that one can't even pin them down in one's memory. The different emotions bring different parts of the face into play. Joy lights up the eyes; the brows seem relaxed; the lips are often slightly parted, slightly smiling. Sorrow dulls the eyes; the muscles around them contract a little; the brows slightly frown; the lips close as if they were repressing a sob. In anger the lips are closed and repressive, too, but tense, perhaps twitching very slightly (as animals' whiskers twitch when they are angry), and the eyes and eyebrows reflect the tension. These are three basic sorts of emotion that the face shows, but often you will find that the eyes alone will convey a great deal to you. You look at someone's eyes and somehow discover some of the thoughts behind them.

This is the sort of thing that one means when in everyday life one talks of an expressive face—a face on which one reads all kinds of unspoken thoughts, which has a silent language of its own. Some people convey almost nothing by facial expression. Do you ever find yourself looking carefully at someone, hoping to discover what he actually means by some formal, careful thing he has said, and find that his face gives no clues as to what he is really thinking, what the deeper significance is behind the spoken word? It makes communication so much more difficult than when you talk to someone whose face always amplifies whatever he says.

Well, onstage (and this goes for straight actors or opera singers or close-ups in movies, as well as for dancers) the really good mime will have enormous control over his facial expression. He will, in fact, be able to stand on stage, doing absolutely nothing, and convey to an audience in a large theater what he is thinking. It sounds like a miracle, and in a way it is.

Of course, there are certain contributory elements that help. To go back to this simple little scene of Swanilda—we in the audience know that Franz is her sweetheart, that he is blowing kisses to another girl, so that we are not unprepared for Swanilda to be furious when she finds out. But if she is a good mime, she can convey to us not only fury but various other emotions. She can show either contempt or ironic amusement at the fact that he is getting no response from Coppélia; she can convey that she'll get even with him later or that she doesn't really care (though, of course, we know she does)—and all this, not through conventional gestures or dance, but by her facial expressions.

A little later in the scene, however, we get back to conventional gestures. There is a crowd of peasants in the market square, and the burgomaster is talking to Swanilda and Franz. He has pointed to the church on the backdrop and has made the marriage gesture, which tells us he is talking about their getting married. There is an interruption; hammering noises come from the old toymaker's house (actually from the orchestra pit, of course), and some of the peasants look scared. The burgomaster explains that Coppélius is merely making his dolls. He points to Coppélius' house; then with both hands he outlines in front of him two stiff, formalized curves, one below the other, and then gestures with bent elbows in the way that a mechanical doll moves its arms. This curving gesture is a variant of another we see sometimes, used instead of the half-circle around the face for a beautiful person—a gesture outlining the shape of an hourglass. This represents a beautiful woman's figure—and whether or not this is the sort of figure we think beautiful by present-day standards, it is the conventional stage gesture, deriving from the days when curves above and below a narrow waist were the ideal for a woman.

All the peasants seem relieved at the burgomaster's explanation, and Swanilda amplifies it mischievously. She points to Coppélius' house, walks a step or two with bent legs and back like an old man, indicates the doll's shape and the hammering with which the burgomaster has ended his explanation, and then points to her forehead and moves her head and forefinger gently in a negative gesture from one side to another. This tells her friends that the old man who makes the dolls is not quite right in the head.

Coppélius, however, is by no means as crazy as they think. When they have gone away, he comes out, locks his door, points to himself, to the inn across the stage, and makes the drinking gesture. Then he points to the window where Coppélia had been sitting, indicates Franz's actions of blowing kisses and bowing, and makes the universal, everyday gesture of dismissing something as idiotic—raising his hand and moving it sharply downward as if hitting a ball with the palm of it.

He goes off to have his drink, but on the way the village boys jostle him, and in the upset he drops his key. Swanilda and her friends come in, and one of them finds it. She spreads out her hands, asking Swanilda what she thinks. Swanilda touches her forehead with her forefinger, meaning thought —in this particular context, "I've got an idea!" Then she points to Coppélius' door, stretches out her hand with the key in that direction, turning her wrist as if turning the key in the lock, and looks inquiringly at her friends. They have mixed reactions—some shake their heads firmly; others nod eagerly. She leads them in, even though some are reluctant.

One thing that emerges when one considers mime is how much is done by pointing. Obviously, if dancers were to be told as children used to be, "It's rude to point," or if they had the temperament of Gary Cooper, who claimed that even pointing without raising one's arm was embarrassingly demonstrative, and that a thumb jerk was sufficient, the whole structure of narrative mime would collapse. But what one doesn't realize, until one watches it onstage, is how graceful and expressive pointing can be, and also how varied.

Notice the difference between the way dancers point onstage and the way ordinary people point in everyday life. When any of us are asked a direction, what do we do—that is, if we point out the place? We lift an arm, bent at the elbow, and extend the forefinger; sometimes we straighten out the arm, sometimes not. But when a dancer points, the gesture is based on the classical positions of the arms and controlled by technical training and musical rhythm just as much as if it were a dance step, and the result is beautiful to look at.

One of the factors that can give shades of meaning to the gesture of pointing is timing, and there is an example of this in Act II of *Coppélia*. Swanilda discovers that Coppélia is a doll, and when Coppélius returns unexpectedly, she hides by changing clothes with the doll. Franz, climbing through the window, finds Coppélius at home and is given drugged wine by the old man, who wants to try to transfer life from Franz to Coppélia. He thinks he has succeeded, because Swanilda pretends to be the doll come to life.

She questions Coppélius about the other dolls, pointing in turn to the Chinese, the Crusader, the Spanish, and Scottish dolls, and then holding out her hands in inquiry. Coppélius repeats the pointing and gestures as the burgomaster did in Act I—the doll movement and the hammering, preceded this time by the "me" gesture. Swanilda, mischievously, because she knows perfectly well that the drugged Franz sitting by the table is *not* a doll, repeats the pointing and includes Franz. Coppélius answers by pointing to each doll in turn, pausing, and then forcefully and deliberately pointing at

Franz ("and *that* one!"), before he repeats that they all are
dolls he has made.

Swanilda is enraged by the lie, and Coppélius has the
bright idea of suggesting that she do a Spanish dance, with
the fan and mantilla from the Spanish doll, and the gesture
for dance here (and elsewhere in *Coppélia*) is not our old
friend from the serious ballet, the hands twisted over the
head. Coppélius raises his arms and then hops onto the right
foot, with the left crossing in front, repeating the position in
reverse.

All his efforts to distract Swanilda from Franz are, of
course, unavailing. In the end she manages to wake him and
convince poor Coppélius that his doll has never come to life.
She and Franz go off gaily, while Coppélius sinks to his knees
beside Coppélia's chair.

From all this, you can see the categories into which mime
resolves itself. There is the mime which is straight mimicry
of action or of personal idiosyncrasy. There is the mime
which not only imitates action, but also conveys reactions
and thoughts. These two come into every branch of dancing
and the theater, into children's play, and into our methods
of communication with people when we are in countries
where we don't know the language. Third, there is the mime
which is bound by the discipline of some technique so that
it makes statements by using definite gestures—gesture language, in fact—and this has a very wide range. It stretches
from classical dance techniques all over the world to
American Indian sign language or our methods of communicating with deaf-and-dumb people. Fourth, there is the mime
which is the expression of feeling, not action at all, without
the use of words—acting without speech.

These categories overlap at various points, of course. One

of the most difficult aspects of life, as well as one of the most interesting, is that very few things ever have absolutely clear-cut boundaries.

Mime as it is used in education or in our everyday life falls almost entirely into the first two categories. Straight mimicry comes easily to children, and modern education frequently turns this to good account. If you act out a scene from history or literature or the Bible, you learn and remember the subject matter almost without trying. Then, from the teacher's point of view, it is simpler to plan and rehearse a mime play on one of these themes than to write dialogue and get children to learn and speak it properly. Sometimes one student will recite a narrative poem while the others act it out in mime. In the nineteenth century there was quite a vogue, at local concerts and entertainments that amused people before the motion picture, radio, and television were invented, for someone to give a recitation with accompanying actions or to sing an "action song." Both meant that the spoken or sung words were amplified by stilted gestures, the kind of thing one can still see in some amateur operatic or musical performances.

Simple mime plays, like the ones produced at schools, have a useful and interesting extension for both children and adults. They can work as a type of therapy for people suffering from psychological tensions or repressions, by helping them move more easily, express feelings and emotions, and concentrate on observing others. They have to practice physical relaxation, too. The study of mime, like that of dancing, always begins by limbering up and by true physical relaxation. From that, mimes go on to the physical control of breath and muscle—the ability to dictate to each tiny section of the body just what it should do—and to complete coordination of mind and body. All this preparation of the body, however, has to be, in the long run, the servant of the mind, because mime is preeminently an art in which the mind is the master. It is the mind that plans the effects that move the watcher to tears or laughter, the mind that selects the emotions and feelings that are to be conveyed to the audience. And of course, it is this quality of mind that dictates the standards in the art. Everyone could do the exercises and learn the gestures, and if that were all, everyone would be a great mime. But the grades of mimetic greatness vary according to the intelligence, the powers of communication, and the depth of understanding of the artist.

In fact, when we enter the sphere of great mime, we have to recognize as valid the immense claims made for it by one of the great authorities, Rudolf von Laban, in *The Mastery of Movement:* that it "introduces the spectator to the realities of the inner life" and that it is "the representation of inner movements of feeling and thinking by outer and visible movements." Anyone who has seen it employed by great theatrical artists is bound to accept this. Frequently the great moment of mime in a play, for instance, emblazons itself on the memory every bit as much as the spoken word or the sound of a marvelous voice.

Films rely still more on gesture and silent acting. Those of today are, after all, the direct descendants of the silent films, which encouraged and produced a remarkable generation of mimes and which were directed by men whose instinct for expression and gesture was sharpened by the knowledge that it was their principal method of communicating with the public. The camera could do a great deal by clever shots and tricks and cutting, the piano accompaniment and the captions kept the excitement going and underlined the drama; but in the long run every silent film stood or fell by virtue of the acting, and the acting in silent films was, of course, mime.

Do you ever see revivals of any of the great silent films— *The Birth of a Nation, Intolerance, City Lights, The General, The Sheik?* Sometimes they crop up on television; sometimes a selection of them linked with one particular star is launched as a new film, like *Harold Lloyd's World of Comedy*; sometimes the classic ones are shown by clubs or societies or study groups. Don't miss them if you are interested in mime. They are thronged with magnificent moments and passages, because all the old stars—Charlie Chaplin, Harry Langdon, Mary Pickford, Lon Chaney, and so on—were experts in their field. The camera is such a strict taskmaster that their effects had to be perfect. The control they had over the muscles of their faces, so that they could reflect emotions by the right combinations of reaction from eyes, eyebrows, nose, cheeks, mouth, and chin, strikes one as superb. Buster Keaton even did it by his eyes alone, with an otherwise deadpan expression. Everything is crystal clear. Never for a moment, even without the caption, is one in doubt about what they intend. They have perfected the art of communication without words, and the result is that they have us laughing or crying now just as they did their audiences way back before and after World War I.

Take Chaplin, for instance, in one of his greatest films, *The Gold Rush*, the picture he has said that he wants to be remembered by. It has action, comedy, satire, human feeling, and pathos—not perhaps as much of the last two qualities as, say, *City Lights*, but enough to lift it right out of the Keystone Kops comedy class. The storytelling and the story itself are well knit and amusing. The "lone prospector," out in the Klondike of 1898, meets up with Big Jim McKay and a large bear. They seek shelter from a storm near Big Jim's

38

Charlie Chaplin in *The Gold Rush*

claim, in a cabin which belongs to the villain, Black Larsen. The three men and a dog are stormbound and starving. Larsen manages to get away, while Charlie, the "lone prospector," and Big Jim make their Thanksgiving dinner on stewed boots. After the storm they separate. Big Jim has a fight with Larsen, gets hit on the head, and forgets the way back to the claim. Charlie reaches a typical Klondike township and gets acquainted with Georgia, one of the local belles. He invites her to New Year's dinner; she forgets to come but is remorseful when she remembers. Big Jim finds Charlie, who knows how to reach the claim; so off they go to the cabin again. There is a storm, and they escape by the skin of their teeth when the cabin slips over the side of the precipice. They make their fortunes and meet up with Georgia again on board the ship going back to the States.

Each episode in this straightforward story is, from the cinematic point of view, dealt with in brilliant comedy terms, but although the script, the direction, and the cutting all would merit an audience's continued pleasure and laughter, the film is made great by Chaplin's performance—which is, of course, mime from beginning to end.

Chaplin's early career in England (where he was born) was with the Fred Karno company—a comedy team who played the music halls and whose talents and material were a mixture of knockabout clowning, mime, acrobatics, singing, and dancing. All this equipped him for the "little fellow" he was to make so widely known and loved in later life, and in *The Gold Rush*, clowning, comedy, dance movement, and expressive mime all have their place. It is the great clown who gets blown about by the storm or slides backward and forward with the slipping cabin, who finds his pants falling when he is dancing with his girl and ties them up with a rope that unfortunately has a large dog on the other end. It is the music hall dancer who controls the sequence when he uses two bread rolls stuck on forks to sketch out a step dance on the table to amuse the girl in his dream. And it is the great mime who serves the Thanksgiving dinner of the old boot. It is a classic lesson in mime to see him stewing the boot, testing it, basting, and serving it, delicately removing upper section from sole as if boning a fish, and eating shoelaces like spaghetti. Each stage is perfectly observed and portrayed with complete clarity, so that the original action from which the mime is derived is immediately recognizable.

Chaplin's influence has been enormous, but his art also has its origins in history. From the beginning of time, the mime theater has had certain character types which have allowed for personal variations and embroideries, and there was undoubtedly a harassed but triumphant "little fellow" in Greek and Roman days. Chaplin's characterization is an individual amalgam of the court jester and the roles of Pierrot and of Clown; we must see where all these fit into the history of mime.

Part II

THE CHRONOLOGY OF MIME

So far we have dodged about a good deal, from classical ballet to Oriental dance to the silent film. We must get the chronology of mime a little more clearly defined.

Because of its character as an instinctive part of the makeup of a human being, mime must, of course, have existed in some form as long as recognizable men and women have walked the earth. It must very early have also been a dramatic art used to entertain or interest an audience, just as early, in fact, as the tribal gatherings around the campfires of primitive peoples. We can be sure of this because of what we know of the brilliant mime and mimicry of many African tribes or of Australian aborigines.

The aborigine in Australia is constantly, and rightly, talked of as a Stone Age man. This is because when white men first reached Australia—and even now in those communities which have not come to terms with white Australian influences—the aborigine was a nomadic hunter, using primitive weapons, never building villages or settling down to agriculture or pastoral occupations. Nevertheless, these acceptedly uncivilized people had, and still have, a fascinating dance and mime culture.

At their tribal gatherings, called corroborees, many of

Australian corroboree

their dances are mimicries. They are linked with the religious structure of their society, which groups men under bird or animal totems. The dancers, intricately decorated by designs in pipe clay on their naked bodies, act out the myths of their totems with instantly recognizable, perfectly observed impressions of emus and kangaroos, snakes, lizards, and all kinds of fish and birds. They are not, however, limited to natural history. An example of their ability for human mimicry is quoted in *Walkabout* by Charles and Elsa Chauvel. These film makers spent an evening watching dances and listening to music. At the end there was a surprise number in which the aborigines "took off" the film makers, and as the Chauvels write: "It was not so much the dressing of the parts that intrigued us as the curiously sensitive mime that so exactly belonged to each character portrayal. The movements of our cameraman were unmistakably his, so that even without the makeup we would have recognized the portrayal."

If this is what our Stone Age contemporaries are capable of, it is a fair assumption that people put on mimes for the benefit and amusement of tribal audiences many centuries ago.

All the same, this is only deduction. There is no real evidence. Nor is there real evidence, except what can be gleaned from wall paintings, perhaps, of mimed *entertainment* in the days of the ancient Middle Eastern civilizations. Mime and mimicry, however, were universally employed in religious rites and in honor of the gods.

When we get to Greece and Rome, we are on firmer ground. Aristotle in the *Poetics* writes forcefully about what he terms imitation. "Imitation is natural to man from childhood ... and it is also natural for all to delight in works of imitation." From this it is a short step to an audience delighting in a performance based on imitation—mimicry and its higher developments.

Dance and mime were then, as now, greatly intermingled. The famous Pyrrhic dances of the Greek warriors, for instance, were partly a mimetic representation of different kinds of fighting. Aristotle's definition of dancing, "the representation of actions, characters and passions by means of posture and rhythmic movements," is quite as applicable to mime. Indeed, very often ancient writers mean mime or gesture when they speak of dancing, and of course, it still had religious connotations. Priestesses, those on Apollo's holy island of Delos among others, were renowned as mimes, as well as vocal mimics. It would not be at all surprising if the famous Greek healing centers at Kos or Epidaurus proved to have initiated the therapeutic use of mime for nervous ailments.

The importance of pantomime in Greek drama was underlined by the fact that the number of individual speaking parts in Greek plays was severely limited, and therefore, much of the action had to be wordless. The players had to be proficient in both speech and mime. A famous actor, Telestes, was renowned for his ability to "depict events with his hands." In tragedy, mime took the form mainly of stylized gestures, sometimes accompanying the choral speaking which carries the action forward; the players were called Ethologues. In comedy it was much freer. If you see a modern Greek company perform, say, *The Birds* by Aristophanes in Greek, it is surprising how much of the action you can follow without knowing the language because of the expressiveness of the actors and their use of mime; obviously, similar effects must have been created when the play was new.

At the same time, mime of a highly popular, broadly amusing, and frequently indecent sort was a feature of the performances put on by itinerant companies of jugglers, acrobats, and entertainers all over the Greek-influenced world. Women took part in these, as well as men, and at their best the players were obviously clever and funny; at their worst they overstepped all the bounds of what was acceptable in entertainment. They traveled in small bands, usually with a star performer, the *archimimus* (or, in the feminine, *archimima*), constantly improvising topical episodes, as well as giving popular favorites. There was one slightly macabre employment for an *archimimus*—mimicking the dead. A bereaved family would hire his services to impersonate their relative in his funeral rites. The mime, dressed in the dead man's clothes, imitated his walk and actions and acted out brief incidents from his life. This happened in Rome, as well as in Greece; it is on record that a mime walked in the Emperor Vespasian's funeral procession. Possibly some memory of this custom continued over the centuries and was responsible for funeral mutes, who were still to be seen just before World War I. Dressed in mourning (top hats and frock coats in those days), heavily draped with black crepe, these undertakers' employees walked in the funeral processions miming grief—but that was all they did mime. There was no longer any thought of linking the mime to the character of the dead man.

Greek mime plays fell into two categories. One was a literary form which became quite dissociated from the theater, the other a completely theatrical, popular, and realistic blending of mime, speech, song, and dance. Some of the authors are known. Epicharmus of Sicily lived in the fifth century B.C., and Herodas of the island of Kos in the third century B.C. The mimes spread north from Sicily through Greek territories in Italy, and gradually the element of mime became increasingly important, and instead of amplifying

46

speech, it became an art form on its own. Sometimes a pro-
logue was spoken, perhaps partly to take the place of program notes; a mime, after all, would rarely be completely
self-explanatory. Unless it dealt with a universally known
tale of some popular god or hero, the audience would need
an outline of the action. Fragments of mimes exist; they may
be a mixture of what was spoken and what was simply background material from which the artists worked.

For instance, if one studies mime today, some of the handbooks give synopses of mime plays which read rather like
pieces of ordinary plays. They are not at all unlike the Greek
mime *The Faithless Wife*, which exists in a papyrus of the
second century B.C. and which is quoted in the original and in
translation in William Beare's *The Roman Stage*. This gives
a list of characters; then, under scene numbers, it lists brief
sections of dialogue or, more frequently, monologue, which
unfold the very sketchy story. It is about a rich woman who
orders a slave to be poisoned because he does not return
her love, together with a female slave whom he loves, and
who also plans to poison her old husband. Her designs are
thwarted, and only drugs are administered. Although the
dialogue sections sound as though the chief mime spoke the
lines, I suspect this may not have been so. Outlines of contemporary mimes are sometimes written in this way so that
the mime tackling the part is helped by knowing the sentiments that lie behind her gestures, expressions, and actions.

All the same, what remains of these early mimes does not
fit in exactly with this theory, so that possibly some spoken
dialogue alternated with passages of silent acting. There was
no reason then, as now, why theatrical forms should not be
mixed together in different proportions on different occa-
sions. Silent acting, or acting by using a gesture language, is
mime, whether it has additional explanations in print or ac-

companying song or speech. The mime passages in these ancient performances would not necessarily be extempore either, as some authorities seem to think; they may well have been choreographed and committed to memory by the actor and reproduced exactly on each occasion, even if no written record suggests this.

In Rome the completely silent mime climbed to immense popularity. To have plays totally without words was a novelty, and the Romans were great seekers after novelty in entertainment. Mimes were easily followed, too, and appreciated by the wide cross section of the Roman public who thronged the theaters. The rulers approved them: Julius Caesar took a mime company with him on his campaigns; Augustus was an enthusiast, Nero a performer. Players—the tragic ones were called *pantomimi,* the buffoons *mimi*—became household words. One, Livius Andronicus, who was also an actor and writer, is sometimes credited with initiating the whole genre by playing a part silently when he lost his voice on one occasion; more probably he merely discovered his talent for mime through such a mishap.

Some people think the origins of the Roman mimes lie in the Middle East, particularly in Egypt, not in Greece and Sicily. Obviously, however, influences were constantly being exchanged and felt throughout the whole territory, and it would be impossible to track them down with any exactness. The links between Greece, Rome, and North Africa were immensely close at this date. If one looks at a New Testament map showing the great cities visited by St. Paul and the Apostles, it becomes very clear how easily travelers could move by sea and land around the eastern Mediterranean. Then, as now, theater people were nomadic—they lived where they could find work and moved somewhere else if it seemed a good idea. This was the case with actors of spoken drama, because Greek and Latin were universally spoken throughout the Roman Empire, but even more the case, of course, with dancers and mimes, whose art had no barriers. As a result, Roman mimes were performed in Egypt, in Sicily (where many of the *Greek* players had originated—a Syracusan called Sophron was one of the first inventors of mimes), in the Roman domains of Spain, and in the south of France, as well as throughout Italy and Rome; Greek mimes may well have had their effect on the mimed story-telling and improvised plays which grew up and continued to flourish among the peoples of Asia Minor and North Africa; and two of Rome's most famous composers of pantomime in the time of Augustus came from these territories: Bathyllus from Alexandria and Pylades from Cilicia.

Pylades specialized in the creation of tragic pantomimes, while Bathyllus was celebrated for comedies. They went into management together in Rome about 22 B.C., and the pantomime flourished as a result. Inevitably, however, disagreements and jealousies set in, factions of rival supporters were created and began to fight it out in the streets, so at last the two broke up their partnership.

The Roman writer Lucian of Samosata, who lived in the second century A.D., dealt at length with pantomimes. He listed a great many mythological and legendary themes and told anecdotes of the players. Sometimes, according to his memory, they "exceeded the due limits of mimicry." Once, he recalls, a player got so carried away in playing the role of a madman that he seemed himself to lose his wits. His crazy acting horrified "the politer sort" in his audience; the "riffraff . . . couldn't distinguish good from bad but considered that sort of thing a consummate mimicry." There is,

of course, always the danger that overexaggerated playing
will be praised and really sensitive subtle mime ignored.

Lucian, in this admirable essay *On Pantomime,* enlarged
on a fascinating and very probable theme—that Proteus, who
is claimed in legend to be able to take on many different
shapes, was in reality a great mime. The translation of this
passage in Jack Lindsay's book *Leisure and Pleasure in
Roman Egypt* runs as follows:

> It seems to me that the ancient myth about Proteus the
> Egyptian means nothing else than that he was a dancer, an
> imitative fellow, able to shape and change himself into any-
> thing, so that he could imitate even the liquidity of water and
> the sharpness of fire in the vivacity of his movement; yes, the
> ferocity of a lion, the rage of a leopard, the quivering of a
> tree—in short, anything he wished.

He goes on about great mime:

> The dancer undertakes to enact characters and emotions,
> introducing now a lover and now an angry person, a man
> afflicted with madness, another with grief, and all this within
> set limits. Indeed the most astonishing thing is that on one
> day we are shown Athamas in a frenzy, then the next mo-
> ment Ino in terror; presently the same person is Atreus, and
> soon after Thestes; then Aigisthos or Airope. Yet they are all
> only a single man.

The history of mime is full of men (and some women)
who are capable of this kind of miracle. In our own century,
for instance, to take three more or less at random, there have
been classical ballet artists like Vaslav Nijinsky, who could
create the savage golden slave in *Scheherazade* and the suffering puppet of *Petrushka;* Adolph Bolm, the sensitive
Pierrot of *Carnaval* and the fierce Polovtsian chief of *Prince
Igor;* or, much more recently, Robert Helpmann, who could
turn from the tragic drama of *The Rake's Progress* to the

outrageous comedy of a stepsister in *Cinderella*. These are indeed the heirs of Proteus.

At its best, therefore, the art of pantomime in Roman days was excellent indeed. Unfortunately, with the other arts, it was to decline. Its popularity was its undoing— it became increasingly vulgar and indecent in theme and action, as it pandered to the lowest public taste, and not unnaturally, as the Christian church became established, it fought against spectacles which were, more and more, reflecting and encouraging depravity. The vogue for mimes gradually diminished, although after the power of Rome in the West faded, there was still for a time a public for these performances at the Byzantine court of Rome in the East, at Constantinople. In fact one dancer-mime (she was not very famous in this capacity), Theodora, became an empress by marrying the Emperor Justinian in the sixth century A.D.

Outside Europe and the Middle East, dramatic mime also flourished. Frequently dance, mime, and drama had religious origins, as in India, and usually mime predated drama and then continued to exist as a parallel theatrical art.

Dance drama (*nātya*) in India goes back to that country's earliest civilization, when Hindu belief maintains that the god Brahma invented it, feeling that the ordinary man needed an art which would have no barriers of appreciation. Its first great teacher was the wise man Bharata Muni, so it became known, and is still known, as *Bharata-nātya*.

Mime is only one part, although the most important perhaps, of Bharata-nātya. A typical program begins with pure dancing, reflections of music and rhythm, an impression of swaying arms and body, swinging, brilliantly colored costume drapes, tinkling ankle bells; only in the third and fourth sections, the *sabdam* and the *varnam*, does it reach mime plays rich in significant gesture, usually interpreting and accompanying songs. The movement and gestures, for which a dancer uses eyes, eyebrows, and neck, as well as head, body, and limbs, were completely worked out and recorded in an encyclopedic work in Sanskrit known as Bharata's *Principles of Dance and Drama.*

These gestures can be made to speak to an audience in a masterly way. There is a very great Bharata-nātya dancer called Balasaraswathi, whose performances in this technique are a revelation. Not beautiful, not particularly young or slender, this woman has such command over her art and such power of communication that one watches, fascinated, as she mimes, and sees every incident as it is recounted by her gestures. Quickly succeeding one another come the happy lover, the jealous wife, the religious penitent, and the doting mother, and where, to start with, was merely a quiet, slightly sullen expression, countless changes of gaiety, liveliness, devotion, or sorrow pass over her face.

At the time of the Roman mimes, Bharata-nātya must have been the reigning mime tradition in India. There was mime, too, in China, which may well have the most ancient pantomime history in the world. A writer who lived in China in 100 B.C. tells us that there was a brilliant mime then called Meng, whose art was admired by one of the king's ministers. After this minister died, his son became very poor. Meng thought of a way to draw the king's attention to the situation, and dressing up in the robes of the dead minister, he impersonated his movements and appearance so perfectly that the king thought the minister had been brought back to life. When he discovered the truth, he offered to make Meng a minister as a tribute to his fine acting, but instead Meng begged for a post for the minister's poor son.

Balasaraswathi (Bharata-nātya, India)

Whether or not Meng was a court jester, many of the early Chinese mimes were entertainers of this kind. They were solo performers, and one of their skills was the acting of short scenes of tragedy or comedy. A man hunting a tiger to take revenge for his father's death, a woman complaining because her husband habitually got drunk and beat her, short excerpts of folk stories or legends—all kinds of subjects made up their repertoire.

Chinese mime was beginning to develop into a tradition of total theater, encompassing all the theatrical arts, by the time of the early Middle Ages in Europe, where the discredited players had taken once more to the roads and the wandering life from which the Greek mimes had emerged. The minstrels and jongleurs of medieval times were the link with past glory, although they had music and storytelling skills, as well as mimetic ability. At court, king's jesters applied their quick wits to satirical mime, as well as to jest and dance, and mime gestures of ancient origin made their way into medieval court dances, such as the branle, and into folk dances such as the morris dance in England.

The wandering players appeared at fairs and festivals, sandwiching interludes of mime into spoken or danced entertainments, because popular attention is always most easily held by variety in a theatrical program. They knew as well as the old strolling players of Greece that the best way to stop unsophisticated audiences from getting bored and moving off was to turn from singing to dancing, from juggling to an acted scene, from mime to tumbling. Mime was particularly useful in the noisy open-air settings in which they performed, in competition with peddlers and quacks shouting their wares or touting for customers.

As time went on, mime also found its place again in dra-

54

matic history. It was a feature of the mystery, miracle, and morality plays that developed in and after the twelfth century in France, Germany, England, and elsewhere and of the mumming plays of the English countryside, about St. George and other folk heroes, whose rituals preserved a certain amount of ancient gesture of a symbolic kind.

Mystery and miracle plays resembled each other closely. The difference simply was that the mysteries took their subjects from the Old and New Testament events, while the miracles dealt with the lives and legends of the saints. The mysteries, as well as dramatizing Christ's life and death like the modern Passion plays, had stirring scenes of the Flood, or Jonah and the whale, or Daniel in the lions' den. All these plays had their origins in Christian religious rituals of the time, when sections of the Bible story were mimed in church to the accompaniment of choral or solo singing. Gradually they emerged from this setting to reach an even wider public out of doors, in market squares or village greens, in fairs or festivals. They had spoken scenes, comedy touches (these became a lot freer and easier, as one could imagine, when they were played outside sacred buildings), music, and mime.

Morality plays were allegories, illustrating morals and full of characters who personified qualities like Good and Evil. The most famous of them, *Everyman,* belongs to a later date —the sixteenth century—but moralities flourished long before that and, even more than the mysteries and miracles, contained mime interludes—often those dealing with hell and that colorful character the Devil.

Religion, which had shaped events so much in the past, made another contribution to the development of European gesture languages. The growth of the great religious orders, Benedictine, Cistercian, and so on, particularly those which required vows of silence, created a complex sign language which is set out in great detail in treatises of the time. For the most part, these gestures dealt with daily life—food and clothes—and with specific words used in rituals and services. Some of the gestures described have striking similarities to those used in classical ballet mime, particularly some action gestures such as to sleep or to write. Probably a good deal of exchange went on in the world of gesture between monks and itinerant players; monasteries of old, with their function as givers of hospitality to travelers, had very close links with the day-to-day life of the people.

While the miracle, mystery, and morality plays were in vogue in Europe, other dance drama traditions were continuing.

In Japan, the *nō* drama, combining a gesture language with its sung and intoned text, became famous under the shoguns of the fourteenth and fifteenth centuries. The mime element in *nō* derived largely from a type of performance, brought to Japan from Korea in the seventh century, that seems to have resembled the Greek and Roman satirical pantomimes and dances—and it is almost irresistible to wonder whether the influence had stretched right across the world. Mime was also involved in a popular variety entertainment known as *saragaku*, which reached Japan from China in the eighth century. This often took the form—comic solo miming—that the Chinese court jester specialized in. The Japanese term for mime is *mono-mane*. Once a great many character types were included in these mimes, but in the fourteenth century one of the great figures in Japanese theater history, Se-ami Motokiyo, decided that all these varying types sprang from three basic roles: an old man; a woman; a warrior. Since then only three forms have been recognized

Nō theater, Japan

in *nō*. In Se-ami's view a mime must identify himself so closely with his part that he should feel himself to *be* that part, which is a very modern conception of acting.

The *nō* plays went on perfecting their style until the seventeenth century. This form of theater is of immense interest to the student, because one can really watch, in the twentieth century, a performance that looks almost exactly as it must have done to seventeenth-century viewers. The *nō* theater is very much "caviare to the general," as Hamlet, a seventeenth-century Westerner, would say. A typical performance is exceedingly static—even more so than the first act of *Tristan and Isolde*—and it is full of apparently outlandish sounds and combinations of sound that come either from the star performer or from a small group of singers and musicians, with words that not even all modern Japanese necessarily understand, so it is by no means an easy entertainment. To some people it is a fascinating escape from the present day; to others it is merely soporific. Its relation to mime is mainly by reason of the gesture technique very sparingly used in its serious episodes and by the action of its comedy interludes.

The fact that the *nō* dramas grew so static and became so much a special, rather highbrow type of theater inevitably meant that a more popular form of dance drama began to develop in Japan. Surprisingly, perhaps, it is supposed to have begun with a woman, which makes it unusual in theater history. She was O Kuni of Izumo, a temple dancer who was a contemporary of Shakespeare's and whose dancing and mime originated the *kabuki* dance theater.

Kabuki today is represented by a number of different companies—some of them either all-male or all-female in personnel; some predominantly dance companies; others, like the Chinese classical companies, a form of total theater.

Tsuchigumo—"The Spider" (Azuma Kabuki, Japan)

Some of their dance dramas are adaptations from *nō* theater plays. Often they are grim stories with supernatural themes. There is one, for instance, about a monstrous spider, *Tsuchi-gumo,* who is destroyed by the hero Raiko. The role of the spider is full of the most haunting menace and very much emphasized by a magnificently sinister costume. The intensity of feeling of which Japanese actors are capable is boundless. On the other hand, they can be amusing, as in the interludes of the *nō* plays, such as the one about three fraudulent beggars who are pretending to be crippled, blind, and deaf, but who are found out. As with the Chinese, when the Japanese play comedy, there are no frontiers to appreciation—their comic mime is beautifully timed, brilliantly observed, and thoroughly enjoyable.

In India, other forms of dance drama were emerging. Nowadays there are a good many schools of classical dance technique in India and Pakistan, most of them with dance drama traditions, of which the most important (apart from Bharata-nātya) are probably *kathakali, kathak, manipuri,* and the recently revivified *kuchipudi.*

Kathakali, which is basically a product of the seventeenth century, is one of the most fascinating. Two neighboring rajas were enthusiastic connoisseurs of dance and mime, and they composed religious mimes in rivalry with each other. The most popular were about the hero Rama and were the forerunners of the dance drama we can still see, in all its marvelous color and vigor.

Again, the kathakali is a dance drama of a specialized taste, although not perhaps as specialized as the *nō* theater. It combines singing, instrumental music, a modicum of dance, and a maximum of mime and gesture language, and it is native to the southwestern coastal district of Malabar. Its themes are religious, drawn from the great Sanskrit epics of the *Rāmāyana* and the *Mahābhārata*, but they are not limited to serious drama and tragedy; there is a strong comedy element, which shows itself particularly in very naturally observed characterizations, among which are some very endearing villains.

The kathakali company of Kerala Kalamandalam, the most widely known group performing kathakali dance dramas, has by touring given the world outside India a chance of coming to grips with this technique. One of the oldest dramas in its repertoire is a play based on the *Rāmāyana*. At home in Kerala, the story unfolds itself over hours of performance; the version we see in the West is confined to a selection of scenes.

The excerpt opens with the villains, a demon king and his uncle, discussing a plot to abduct Rama's wife Sita and carry her off to their stronghold in Ceylon. Immediately you are aware that in spite of a very specialized technique, or perhaps because of it, these mime actors have immense resources of expression and full-blooded acting ability. They look superhuman, in magnificently colored costumes with full skirts and gorgeous headdresses, their faces made up in the most brilliant colors and designs. All the colors and patterns have significance. A basic green, to which white and black is applied, is the color for heroes and gods. The addition of red creates a demon. Red beards signify villains (there is an interesting parallel here with Von Rothbart—Redbeard—in our Western *Swan Lake*), while white beards belong to some superhuman characters like the marvelous monkey god, Hanuman. A golden-yellow makeup base is for women (played always by men) and holy men, representing gentleness and spirituality.

The demons in the *Rāmāyana* get off to a good start with a plot that is easily understandable—not the details, of

Kathakali company of Kerala Kalamandalam, India, in
Rāmāyana

course, because these are contained in the rapid flow of gesture language with which their astonishingly eloquent hands converse. They take an obvious and very enjoyable delight in planning their villainous designs. Then we switch to a group of three: Rama, his brother Lakshmana, and Sita, traveling through the forest. The demons send a magic deer to distract Rama, who is a hunter. It is so beautiful (we see it only through the descriptive gestures of the actors) that Sita begs Rama to catch it for her as a playmate. He stalks it, in an expressive solo, trying over and over again to entice it with handfuls of grass so that he can take it to Sita.

Meanwhile, Sita becomes worried about Rama and sends his brother to look for him. So she is defenseless when the demon king sweeps down and carries her, protesting, to his winged chariot. This is a large green wooden block—the only type of prop used. The demon lifts Sita onto it, where she stands in abject fear, he holds her with one arm, and they both fall into a convincing rhythmical swaying motion as the invisible chariot takes the air.

Suddenly the king of the birds, a friend of Rama's, swoops in to try to save Sita. He and the demon circle together, the bird using beak and wings, the demon his short sword. At last the demon strikes off the bird's wings. Fatally wounded, the bird manages to tell Rama and Lakshmana what has happened before he dies.

Rama seeks the help of a monkey prince, Sugriva, who agrees to give it on condition that Rama kills Sugriva's brother Bali with whom Sugriva has a deadly feud. In the next scene we see the monkey princes quarreling. This is immensely funny. The actions of monkeys are closely followed, also their chattering—sometimes violently aggressive, sometimes petering out in intermittent whimpers (Oriental and Indian mimes are never afraid to make vocal noises;

unlike Western mimes, they are rarely totally silent). They break off their squabbles, pretend to be uninterested, eat, scratch, look around—and then start all over again. There is an air of almost good-natured family squabbling, so that it comes as something of a shock when Rama, true to his promise to Sugriva, enters with his bow and shoots Bali dead.

The excerpt ends with Bali's long-drawn-out dying (kathakali mimes delight in the gruesome and horrific, as well as the subtle and splendid) and the mourning of his family, but it is interesting to know that in the story the monkey people eventually build a bridge to Ceylon and help Rama recover Sita.

All this, performed with vigor and pleasure, has not changed much since the seventeenth century. The training and exercises which build up the technique, the traditional costumes, makeup, and music belong to the past as much as to the present, but as drama without words, it shows the full expressiveness that mime can achieve.

Linked to the kathakali and other Indian dance dramas are those of Ceylon, but they have a different form. Instead of recounting continuous stories from the great epics, they are usually made up of passages of pure dancing (devil dances and elephant god dances are the most famous) alternating with unrelated mime interludes. These serve the same purpose as the Greek and Italian ones, sometimes introducing a comic element, satirical or farcical or bawdy, or amplifying the themes of religious exorcism by recounting traditional stories connected with the devil dances of the past. The mime is largely silent acting, in which perhaps a male player will portray a woman engaged in her daily work and life by closely observed manners and ways, rather than "speak" dialogue made up of precise and complicated hand and finger gestures.

As old as these dance drama traditions is that of Thailand. It has two branches. Rather in the way that kabuki is the popular form deriving from the *nō* plays in Japan, so *lakhon* is a later and more popular form of theater in Thailand than *khon*. The khon is ancient, influenced by India, and takes its themes exclusively from the *Rāmāyana*. As with kathakali, all the actors are men. Unlike kathakali, masks are used, instead of elaborate masklike makeup. Lakhon, which has practically superseded khon (whereas *nō* and kabuki exist side by side), really has two sections as does kabuki—pure dance troupes and dance drama companies. Both are mainly composed of women, and a far wider range of subject matter is tackled than by the old royal entertainment of khon. Cambodia, close geographically, has a royal dance drama tradition, while Java and Bali have complicated repertoires of dance dramas based on the Sanskrit epics. Mime played its part, too, in the construction of the great religious drama festival of Tibet.

Long before the seventeenth century, Europe had seen the start of a vitally important theatrical movement. Characters with some similarity to those of the ancient Roman mimes were appearing in a new form. Some authorities believe that the link between the Pappus, Maccus, and Bucco of Roman days and the fifteenth-century Pantaloon, Clown, and Punchinello is firm and complete; others see little or no connection between them. This is exactly the sort of contradiction that flourishes among historians—almost always, there are two schools of thought. It seems reasonable, however, to think that some handed-down tradition, probably more than

Traditional dance drama, Thailand

half-forgotten, was given new and independent life in the hands of the talented Italian and Sicilian players in these fascinating plays in which mime was featured, even if speech was the predominant ingredient. And along with these possible descendants of Roman characters came another—Arlecchino (or Harlequin). His origins are even more ancient. He is a memory of the god Mercury. His skullcap derives from the cap of invisibility, his wand from the caduceus, his brilliant dancing from the speed of Mercury's winged sandals, and in Harlequin plays through the centuries he has been a potent magician, reflecting Mercury's magic powers.

This type of Italian play was called a *commedia dell'arte all'improvviso*—a comedy improvised by professional actors. Shortened to commedia dell'arte, this title is famous as a genre of theater and as a theatrical tradition. Its influence spread all through Europe in the sixteenth century, all the more easily because some of the action was mimetic and improvised. A long list of plays was woven around this set of popular characters, the most famous of which are known to us as Harlequin, Pierrot, and Columbine; one play after another was given over the years, rather in the way that we now have television series dealing with familiar people—the Dr. Kildares and Perry Masons of our TV entertainment.

When the commedia dell'arte spread to France, mime took on greater importance. The companies that performed these plays were the actors, called *forains,* who appeared at the great fairs—the Foire de Saint-Germain or the Foire de Saint-Laurent. They acted out of doors, on long narrow stages, and because their lively nature made the more formal theatrical productions of Paris seem dull to audiences, the authorities decided to forbid spoken plays to be given at the fairgrounds. As a result, of course, mime flourished. At first, scrolls covered with explanatory verse were shown as an accompaniment to the mimes (this custom is remembered when Marcel Marceau's assistant shows us a card bearing the title of the coming scene), and when this, too, was forbidden, printed synopses were handed around among the spectators. This naturally led to developments in the already established gesture conventions of the commedia dell'arte. These mimes, along with traditions from the miracle and morality plays and gestures from the court ballets and from that complex entertainment the masque (which included something of practically everything theatrical) laid the foundations for the gesture language of Western classical ballet and pantomime.

In England, another form of mime became popular—the dumb show. This began as a silent scene preceding each act of a spoken play, forming an introduction and bringing life and movement into an otherwise rather static entertainment. This was how it was used in *Gorboduc* (*c.* 1560), one of the earliest tragedies in English literature. From then on, about seventy plays are recorded to have included some form of dumb show. Gradually it changed its character. It developed into a more integral part of the play. First of all, it merely forecast some aspect of the plot, but soon it began to be about the characters of the play, and at last it actually carried forward the action by presenting a scene of importance.

Most of these dumb shows are irrelevant to the theater today; their point has perished with the ephemeral plays that brought them about. One or two, however, are linked with dramas that are still of vital importance, as is the one in *Hamlet*.

This comes when Hamlet is trying to find evidence that Claudius has murdered his father—trying, in fact, to make

Claudius reveal his guilt. The players arrive, and Hamlet has the sudden idea that he will have them "play something like the murder of my father before mine uncle" and see if this shakes Claudius into a confession. The dumb show, with its subsequent spoken echo, is the result.

Imagine the setting. The court of Elsinore has gathered in the great hall of the castle to see the play. King Claudius, the big, bluff, genial murderer, sits with his wife, Queen Gertrude, Hamlet's mother. Old Polonius, the chief minister, is there, expecting to be bored. The sycophantic Rosencrantz and Guildenstern and the other courtiers settle in their places, half-blasé, half-willing to be amused. Hamlet's friend Horatio is in a position where he can see Claudius—Hamlet has urged him to this, telling him about the trap he has set for the king. Ophelia sits close to Hamlet, gravely disturbed by his odd behavior, trying to behave as if everything were as usual. She is the one who crystallizes the point about the dumb show: "Belike this show imports the argument of the play."

Now, to quote the first folio (that is, the first authoritative edition of Shakespeare, published in 1623):

> The dumb shewe enters. Enter a King and Queene, very lovingly; the Queene embracing him. She kneeles, and makes shewe of Protestation unto him. He takes her up, and declines his head upon her neck. Layes him downe upon a Banke of Flowers. She seeing him asleepe, leaves him. Anon comes in a Fellow, takes off his Crowne, kisses it, and pours poyson in the King's eares, and Exits. The Queene returnes, findes the King dead, and makes passionate Action. The Poysoner, with some two or three Mutes, comes in againe, seeming to lament with her. The dead body is carried away; the Poysoner woos the Queene with Gifts, she seems loath and unwilling awhile, but in the end accepts his love. Exeunt.

The dumb show from John Gielgud's modern dress
production of *Hamlet*

You see, the playwright says all that is necessary about what the dumb show is meant to represent. On the other hand, it is left to the actors or (in our time) the director to decide how this clear instruction is to be carried out—where the players are to stand, what gestures they are to use to convey to the audience what the playwright intends. There are alternative ways of doing even the simplest of these required actions: to come in, to kiss, to lie down. Shakespeare is not concerned with *how* the actors do them, merely that they should be done and that they should clearly tell the audience what he wants them to know. From a phrase he puts into Hamlet's mouth, "inexplicable dumb shows," he obviously did not think Elizabethan dumb shows were universally models of clarity! That is hardly surprising because in fact, they must have varied tremendously with the talents of the actors concerned. The scenario (it was called the platt) was pinned up in the actors' greenroom, and they invented their own dumb show to match it.

This dumb show in *Hamlet* exactly forecasts the spoken play within a play that follows, but other dumb shows actually describe plot developments that are only briefly referred to in speech. Two of these come in John Webster's *The White Devil*. The Duke of Brachiano, who is in love with the White Devil (the fascinating Vittoria Corombona), hears from a necromancer how his own wife and Vittoria's husband, Camillo, have been murdered. The necromancer shows him two mimed scenes. In one, Camillo has his neck broken as he is vaulting over a horse at a gymnastic exercise; in the other, the duchess is killed by poison. Webster was a little doubtful of leaving an important part of the action to the mercies of the dumb show—perhaps in case the audience failed to look at it properly. He makes Brachiano say, "Yet each circumstance I taste not fully," so that the necromancer can briefly describe what we have seen—but the description *is* only a brief précis.

These dumb shows sound dull in print, but they seem different when they are staged. When I saw *The White Devil* some years ago, these two murders, mimed, with a slight musical background, and watched by the duke and the necromancer, as well as by the audience, made a memorable counterbalance to the spoken play and heightened greatly the sinister effect. Nightmares are silent—and these took on something of that quality, rather in the way that long passages of silent acting, with an accompaniment of music, always key up the tension in a suspense film.

The dumb show was mainly an English development of mime and was limited to the Elizabethan and Jacobean stage, in contrast with the commedia dell'arte which was so widely dispersed in terms of both geography and time.

A significant date in the development of mime came in France in 1708. The Duchesse de Maine, one of the great ladies of the Sun King Louis XIV's court, sponsored a ballet-pantomime at her château at Sceaux near Paris. This was an entirely mimed scene, to specially composed music, based on a tragic excerpt from Corneille's play *Les Horaces,* and two celebrated dancers of the time performed it. They were Ballon (from whose name classical ballet derives its term for the springy quality in dancing, for which he was especially noted) and Françoise Prévost.

The novelty had its effect, not only at the time but on later developments. Prévost taught her art to her pupils; among them were the great ballerinas Sallé and Camargo, and through Sallé the strands of French and Italian mime and its history in England were drawn together.

This happened because in 1717 a Harlequin was launched

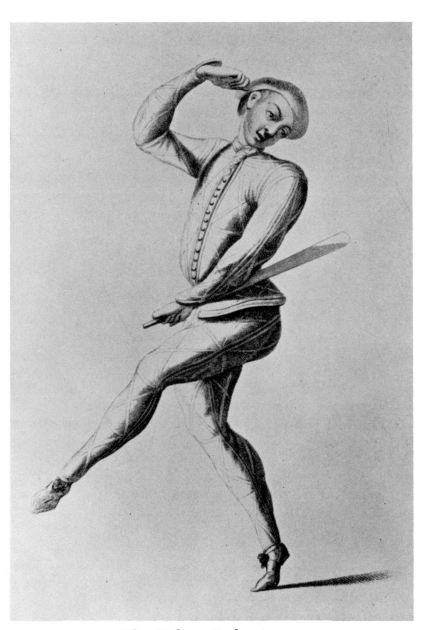

John Rich as Harlequin

in London—by no means the first in England but undoubtedly the most popular and famous. He was an Englishman, John Rich, an actor-manager who inherited from his father a theater in Lincoln's Inn Fields, and his Harlequin plays drew the town for years. Rich made them entirely into mimes. Lacking the voice of an actor, he turned this shortcoming into an asset and was supremely successful. In the company he gathered at Lincoln's Inn Fields he included Marie Sallé. Very young, very talented, Marie Sallé was particularly valuable from Rich's point of view. She had had her basic experience of the theater with her uncle, Francisque Molin, a notable Harlequin of the fairground companies in France, and she had studied dancing and mime with Françoise Prévost.

These pantomimes at Lincoln's Inn Fields were rather like a combination of two plays—one serious and one comic—followed through in alternate acts. For the stage Rich called himself Lun, and the great actor David Garrick, a contemporary of his and a fine exponent of the expressive mime that illuminates spoken acting, rhymed in his praise:

> When Lun appeared, with matchless art and whim
> He gave the power of speech to every limb.

But he had rivals in composition, if not in performance. Colley Cibber, in his *Apology for My Life*, was bitter about the "childish pantomimes" that had taken "so gross a possession of the stage," but he went on to praise one that Rich did *not* originate—*Mars and Venus:* "The whole story was so intelligibly told, by a mute narration of gesture only, that even thinking spectators allowed it both a pleasing and a rational entertainment."

Now this mimed play of *Mars and Venus* was produced,

also in 1717, at the Drury Lane Theatre by John Weaver. Weaver was an English dancing master who probably composed the first mimed play recorded in England, *The Tavern Bilkers,* in 1702—he claimed this honor anyway. In 1712 he wrote an essay on dancing and in 1728 published another book, *The History of Mimes and Pantomimes.* Weaver in England and the ballet masters Hilverding and Angiolini on the continent of Europe in many ways preceded the revolutionary ideas on ballet held by the famous Jean Georges Noverre, but Noverre's influence, through his work in various countries and at various courts and through the publication in 1760 in France of his *Letters on Dancing and Ballets,* was infinitely more widespread.

Noverre, like Weaver, thought highly of the art of pantomime. For him, as for many other people during the history of ballet, the peak of balletic possibility comes when dance and drama combine in a production. It is not a popular view nowadays, when the dance content is the most admired; but in 1760 Noverre deplored the divorce that had come about between pure dancing and pantomime, and in his ballets (which were immensely successful) he "dared"—in his own words—"to reunite action with dancing; to accord it some expression and purpose." On the other hand, he stressed (he was an eminently sane and sensible thinker) that gestures needed to be implemented by real feeling and dramatic expression. Of one man's ballet he wrote: "If it failed to succeed it was due not to any lack of gesture, for his actors' arms were never at rest; nevertheless his pantomimic exhibitions were as cold as ice."

This is exactly what you notice when you compare a basic gesture in class with the same gesture done in context by a fine actor-dancer. "A dancer's arms," wrote Noverre, "will speak in vain if his face be unmoved."

75

As the eighteenth century wore on, this interest and concern for dramatic content grew paramount—not only in ballet but, through the innovations of the composer Gluck, in opera as well. *Ballets d'action*—ballets with dramatic stories told in dance and mime—superseded the Harlequin pantomimes in popularity in England and rose to favor everywhere else in Europe. Each choreographer who was stimulated by Noverre's ideas added his own contribution. Dauberval initiated the comedy ballet—he was the original choreographer of *La Fille mal Gardée;* Didelot (as well as being fascinated by the mechanics of stage effects) concentrated on the clarity of mimetic gesture; Vigano produced dance dramas of an integrated kind, and the criticisms he received, that his ballets had "too much mime and not enough dancing," have been all too frequently echoed in our own time about contemporary dance dramas.

With the nineteenth century, however, commedia dell'arte traditions once more made themselves felt, in the careers of two supreme and supremely different protagonists for the Pierrot-Clown characters: Jean Gaspard Deburau in France and Joseph Grimaldi in England.

Deburau became famous through the Théâtre des Funambules, which opened in Paris in 1816, just after Napoleon's defeat at Waterloo had reinstated a weak monarchy in France. The name Funambules was a link with the comedians of the Roman pantomime, who were sometimes known as *funambuli.* The theater itself was a cellar in the Boulevard du Temple, seating about seven hundred, and cheap. Deburau and his fellow mimes could use miniature effects and develop the art of facial expression far more than could anyone habitually playing in a large-scale auditorium or arena.

This man, who was identified more with Pierrot than anyone else has ever been, lived from 1796 to 1846—fifty years that linked the French Revolution with early-Victorian England and the United States of Emerson, Whitman, and the war with Mexico. He was born in Bohemia to a family of traveling players and acrobats, who were constantly on the move, backward and forward across a Europe troubled by the Napoleonic Wars, as far east as Turkey. Once settled in Paris after Waterloo, it was a question of poverty and struggling, and the role of the downtrodden Pierrot came perilously near the truth. Perhaps that was why Deburau became so memorably great—because his intensely felt suffering could give his comedy that background of melancholy now closely identified with tragic clowns.

It also brought him stardom and drew very different types of audiences to the Théâtre des Funambules. Deburau was sought after by society, shouted for by his public, and eventually enshrined in history and legend.

Pierrot now took over the immense variety of character that Harlequin had indulged in, but his characterizations were on the whole nearer real life. Harlequin had appeared as exotic, superhuman heroes—Harlequin Necromancer, Harlequin Dr. Faustus, Harlequin Emperor of the Moon. Pierrot, as enacted by Deburau, played with miraculous observation and skill everyday people—street cleaners, photographers, cooks, gardeners, customs officials—but touched them with enlightenment. Kay Dick, in her book *Pierrot,* says: "He was the spirit of the people, changing his mood as they changed their mood."

This Pierrot exalted the role into the poetic, white-faced tragicomic character on which in our own time the French mimes Jean-Louis Barrault and Marcel Marceau have based their famous characterizations Baptiste and Bip and which has been immortalized by painters of the fame of Daumier and Picasso. Deburau and his successors were subtle players,

Les Enfants du Paradis (Jean-Louis Barrault as Deburau)

distilling understanding and sensitive feeling into their often
rather muted performances.

Grimaldi, on the other hand, had to broaden the technique
to be successful. By his individual personality he became the
forerunner of the modern clown tradition in theater and
circus—so much so that clowns are sometimes termed Joeys
in memory of him.

In the commedia dell'arte plays the character who was
the ancestor of Pierrot was called Pedrolino or Pagliaccio.
Pagliaccio is the Italian word for clown, and Clown was the
designation by which the part was often known in England.
It is a confusing word, because in Elizabethan times, clown
was a term for a rustic character with a rather slow sort of
mother wit; but the significance of the name was added to,
and eventually Clown implied the most versatile and comic
player in a production. Nowadays the French word Pierrot
is always used for the role derived from the commedia dell'-
arte, and clown has become mainly associated with the
circus.

Grimaldi's character of Clown was basically in the commedia dell'arte tradition—in fact, his father was another
product of the French fairground, who went to England as
a dancer in the 1750's. Grimaldi's performances were so full
of invention, so gay and lively and brilliantly timed, that audiences flocked to see him and fixed his reputation forever
in the English theater. His career began before he was two
years old, at Sadler's Wells Theatre in 1781, and forty-seven
years later he gave his farewell performance there. Clown
and his antics had, over the years, exhausted his physical
resources. Sometimes he had to wear costumes which made
movement and dancing more fatiguing; as Punchinello, for
instance, he had humps on chest and back, a long-nosed

Mr GRIMALDI, as Clown.

Joseph Grimaldi as Clown

mask, and heavy wooden shoes—and in those days these
things meant weight. Only in modern times have modern
materials eased such burdens. He was in great demand. At
one point, in 1802, he appeared in *The Great Devil,* where
he had nineteen changes of costume and played two parts;
he followed with a burlesque, a harlequinade, and then took
a twenty minutes' walk to Drury Lane Theatre to appear
there. All this, plus one or two accidents, when he broke
bones falling through trapdoors or severely burned his foot
onstage, meant that at too early an age he was crippled and
ill. He was irreplaceable to those who had seen him. Dickens
wrote: "There are no standards to compare him with or
models to judge him by; all his excellences were his own
and there are none resembling them among the pantomime
actors of the present day." R. J. Broadbent in *A History of
Pantomime* describes his variety vividly:

> Let the subject be what it may, it never fails to become
> highly amusing in the hands of Grimaldi. Whether it is to
> rob a pieman or open an oyster, imitate a chimney sweep or
> a dandy, grasp a redhot poker or devour a pudding, take
> snuff, sneeze, make love, mimic a tragedian, cheat his master,
> pick a pocket, beat a watchman or nurse a child, it is all per-
> formed in so admirably humorous and extraordinarily natural
> a manner that spectators of the most saturnine disposition are
> irresistibly moved to laughter.

As Deburau is the precursor of all French and French-
influenced pantomime artists, so Grimaldi is father to all circus clowns of our own time. Circus clowning has to be in
the main mime because of the enormous size of the circus
ring. It is frequently very broad mime indeed, aimed at
amusing a great number of not necessarily sophisticated
spectators—including all the little boys who revel in it. Little

Circus clown, United States—Emmett Kelly

girls perhaps like it less; perhaps they take it too seriously. I remember as a child being taken out in tears of dismay because one clown cut off another's (false) head with an outsize pair of scissors so cleverly that I really thought it had happened.

This kind of clowning is partly slapstick, partly clever tumbling and acrobatics, and not very much mime in its sense of portraying feeling by expression. But it can have subtlety and pathos, as well as broad comedy. Emmett Kelly, for instance, effectively incorporated that element of fighting against hopeless odds that Chaplin used so brilliantly, tackling impossible tasks like sweeping up the spotlight beams. Some clowns, like the great Grock, worked both in the circus ring and in the music hall theater, adapting the scale of their clowning to the larger or smaller audience, while in the U.S.S.R., where the finest circus acts are seen today, the clown tradition is brought to a peak of perfection by the magnificent Oleg Popov, who can command a huge audience in the round by a simple and telling scene. He wanders on, alone, into the great ring, finds a pool of golden glow from a spotlight, and as he looks up at it with joy, unfastening his coat, it becomes the summer sun. He settles down, relaxes, opens a bag, and takes out a picnic—bread and cheese and a bottle of drink. Enjoying the warmth, he lies down, stretching out, his cap over his eyes, to sleep. The spotlight moves off him, and he wakes up cold, shivering, rubbing his hands, buttoning up his coat, and hunts around for the lost sunlight. He finds it on the other side of the ring and begins to relax, but it is fitful and starts to fade. Desperately he tries to scoop it up, to gather it, even a little of it, and stuff it into his bag, but it all slips away. This is mime on different levels, as one gets in the theater—the straightforward practical tale of sun equaling warmth and lack of sun equaling

Circus clown, U.S.S.R.—Oleg Popov

cold, and the deeper significance of somebody opening out
under encouragement and happiness and becoming inhibited
again when faced with discouragement and sorrow.

Grimaldi's art used speech, as well as mime, but another
silent mime tradition was being consolidated at the same
time, that of Denmark. As early as 1798 an Italian mime, Pasqual Casorti, had made an attempt to found a company in
Copenhagen, and he managed to gain a footing in 1800. It
was left to his son, however, to popularize pantomime in
Denmark, and he did it so successfully that it still has a
public.

The Danish Pantomimeteater clings to the old Harlequin
plays, and when you look at them, you look at history. *Harlequin's Mechanical Statue,* for instance, was given by Casorti's company in 1800, and other mimes in the repertoire
have equally old origins. All the stories are in the commedia
dell'arte tradition, of the various adventures of Harlequin
and Pierrot when they try to snatch Columbine from her
strict old father. They lack the brilliant intermingling of
tragedy and comedy of the French Pierrots and the zany in-
ventiveness of the clown, but they are disarming in their
unsophisticated charm. They have the perfect setting—a
little theater in the Tivoli pleasure gardens in Copenhagen,
with a fascinating curtain that looks like a peacock's tail.

Mime in Denmark, however, is not limited to the Pantomimeteater; the repertoire of the Royal Danish Ballet is
rich in mime roles and has a strong tradition of first-class
dancer-mimes. One of these, Niels Bjørn Larsen, has been
director of the Pantomimeteater since 1955.

The nineteenth century saw important developments far
away from Europe, with the establishment of the Peking

Pantomimeteater, Tivoli, Copenhagen, Denmark

Opera, but although this flowering came relatively recently, the repertoire of the classical theater of China is, of course, developed from ancient techniques and traditions. Mime is only one part of this complex theatrical spectacle; it is a combination of music and singing, spoken drama, dancing, acrobatics, mime, and gesture language. Some scenes are mainly sung, others completely mimed; others, particularly battle scenes (like the splendid fight between the monkey god and his supporters and the defenders of heaven), are mostly acrobatics, magnificently timed and executed.

One of the scenes that fascinated everyone who saw it when the company toured abroad is brilliantly planned and performed, sometimes called *The Crossroads* and sometimes *Where Three Roads Meet*. It is the same episode, whichever name it bears, and it is based on a fourteenth-century folk story about how a guest at an inn wakes up in the dark and thinks that the innkeeper is attempting to rob and murder him. He fights back, and another guest, his friend, comes to his aid. The delightful point of the scene is that they all are supposed to be fighting in total darkness. In fact, the stage is brilliantly lit, and the audience can see the whole thing; but so clever is the acting, so well timed and worked out, that it carries complete conviction. It is impossible to believe that the three men can see one another as well as we can see them—they reproduce so perfectly the actions and feelings they would have if they were actually fighting in the dark.

In the West, the Romantic ballet was consolidating the narrative and expressive mime that the eighteenth-century ballet masters had made popular. Almost all the great ballerinas of this era were skillful mimes as well as dancers. The critics of the time emphasize this. Of Fanny Elssler in *La*

The Monkey God (Peking Opera)

The Chronology of Mime

Tarentule, for instance, Theophile Gautier wrote: "She showed with terrifying truth the effects of the poison and the increasingly convulsive character of the victim's dance; the most detailed account, spoken aloud, would not have been so plain as her miming." Of Carlotta Grisi in *Esmeralda,* the London *Times* said: "Nothing could be more exquisitely managed than her pantomime."

The choreographer who created many of their most brilliant mime scenes was Jules Perrot. A fine dancer, once a strolling player and acrobat touring France, his own miming was notable for "perfect rhythm and easy grace" (something of which relatively few dancers are capable), and this seems to have been echoed in his choreography. In his ballets he made use not only of conventional gesture, but of expressive mime. In *Eoline* there was a scene where the heroine had to dance against her will with the villain. The London *Times* reported: "The point of the *pas* is to show the horror with which she is obliged to perform it. The play of Mlle. Grahn's [Lucille Grahn] countenance, denoting repugnance and agony, the struggle to free herself, the despair with which she fell into the arms of her tormentor, were finished to the highest degree." This kind of acting (if one can get the message through the very dated pomposity of the writing!) is very much what we now see in the Royal Ballet's *Romeo and Juliet,* where Juliet dances reluctantly with Paris after Romeo has left her, half-hypnotized, half-repelled, expressing many subtle shades of emotion.

Again, writing about another Perrot ballet, *Catarina,* the same newspaper summed up the ballet master's great personal talent as a mime: "Perrot's pantomime in this ballet is, as usual, inimitable. In the scene where he relates his escape from his pursuers, his gestures convey a silent description which no language could equal."

89

Here, then, was mime playing a very integral part in classical ballet, and this continued throughout the century. Russian dancers, naturally expressive, had happily adopted the idea of the *ballet d'action* from Hilverding. The ballets of Noverre and Didelot consolidated it, and another influence made itself felt strongly in both dancing and mime—that of Italy.

From the time of Vigano, dance drama had had its following at La Scala, Milan; the school there had the title of the Imperial Academy of Dancing and Pantomime, and it grew in importance during the nineteenth century under the directorship of Carlo Blasis. When we come to the 1890's in Russia, the Italian infiltration there is of great interest.

These Italians were virtuoso dancers, but they were also for the most part very fine mimes. Virginia Zucchi in a new production of *La Fille mal Gardée* or Enrico Cecchetti creating Carabosse in *The Sleeping Beauty* set standards which dancers at the Maryinsky Theater in St. Petersburg eagerly matched. Cecchetti, who brought off a fascinating double in *The Sleeping Beauty* by creating the dancing role of the Bluebird, as well as the mimed role of Carabosse, was a fine teacher and the founder of the Cecchetti method of dance training. Like many dancers, he lived to a good age. Cyril Beaumont recalls seeing him come out of retirement to play Carabosse for the Diaghilev Ballet in 1922—one special performance. It marked the fiftieth anniversary of his first leading role.

The opportunity of working with, and learning from, mimes like Zucchi meant a great deal to the Russian dancers and was freely acknowledged by artists like Mathilde Kchessinska (who followed her as Lise) or Paul Gerdt, the first prince in *The Sleeping Beauty,* who was masterly in his expressive use of classical gesture. Russian ballet history tells us of a good many magnificent dancer-mimes. One of the most famous was Vassily Geltser, who created the delightful comedy role of Ivanushka in *The Little Hump-backed Horse.* Apparently he had an enormous range, and outside ballet he had one additional triumph. There was a rather obscure opera of the time, Simon's *The Song of Victorious Love,* in which he played the part of a mute Malay servant. People who found the rest of the opera a complete bore used to turn up for the second act merely to see Geltser.

Mime has, in fact, had its part to play in opera. Before the art form of opera was developed, back in the sixteenth century, actors had mimed a narrative which was sung offstage, but even after this custom was superseded and the singers appeared and acted their parts, they had to make use of musically timed gesture and of expressive acting. This was particularly so in comedy—it is impossible to imagine characters like Figaro and Susanna in *The Marriage of Figaro* or Leporello in *Don Giovanni* being sung without the liveliest of accompaniments in mimed action. In other types of role the balance is fairly even. Some great singers have gained fame without any acting ability whatsoever, but others, like the magnificent Chaliapin, are remembered for the tremendous power of their performances as, for instance, his Boris Godunov.

A number of silent characters occur in opera and are usually mimed by dancers as Geltser mimed his Malay mute, and there have been occasional returns to the idea of miming onstage and singing offstage—but these have been produced as ballets by ballet companies. Probably the most notable of them were Gluck's *Orpheus and Eurydice,* which Ninette de Valois staged with the singers in the orchestra pit and with the action mimed and danced by the Sadler's

Wells Ballet, and Rimsky-Korsakov's *Coq d'Or,* which Fokine choreographed for the Diaghilev Ballet in 1914.

This type of production was the prototype for the film of Offenbach's *Tales of Hoffmann,* in which six of the leading characters mimed their roles, with one interesting difference —they frequently mouthed the words, phrasing them as though they were singing. If you get a chance (and it is sometimes revived), have a look at this film, remembering that all the parts played by Moira Shearer, Robert Help-mann, Leonide Massine, Ludmilla Tcherina, Pamela Brown, and Frederick Ashton are acted in this way.

Mime apart from ballet still existed in the West, and in the field of gesture an interesting development came about in France: François Delsarte launched a rebellion against the stylized and unnatural acting techniques and gestures taught at the Paris Conservatoire, where he had been a student. He set up his own teaching studio and gradually evolved an enormously comprehensive and detailed analysis of movement and gesture. He studied people's reactions and gestures in all kinds of occupations or human events, in happiness or sorrow, success or disaster, and worked out a basis for gesture training which became famous in France between 1839 and 1859.

Delsarte based his system on two laws: the law of correspondence and the law of trinity. The law of correspondence dealt with the way in which the spirit and the body are related to each other—how the actions of the body correspond to the actions of the spirit. This truth becomes, of course, ever more obvious, as we discover nowadays the existence of so many psychosomatic illnesses—physical illnesses which are closely related to emotional stress.

The law of trinity divided the body and its movements

into sets of threes. It cited three zones of the body—the head, the torso, the limbs—and then subdivided these, always into three parts. Ted Shawn's fascinating book *Every Little Movement* investigates all this teaching in detail.

Delsarte's conception of gesture is the widest possible one. He maintains that "nothing is so horrible as a gesture without meaning," but he is thinking not purely of mime gesture, with some specific meaning corresponding to a word or sentence, but also of movement gesture, which may have a general emotional meaning. All good dance choreography employs *this* kind of movement gesture—as, for instance, downward or bending movements to imply sorrow or oppression, upward or stretching movements to imply joy or triumph.

Delsarte did, however, deal explicitly with pantomime as well and gave it an important role to play. To quote Ted Shawn: "Pantomime expresses all possible sensations, conditions, situations, emotions, and also deals with objects, space, and sense of space, and direction."

All these revolutionary ideas had great influence. Delsarte taught singers, actors, and orators, as well as dancers; two of these pupils were to spread the word in very divergent spheres.

Steele MacKaye, a young American, studied with him in 1869—shortly before his death in 1871. MacKaye returned to the United States, having worked out a system of what he called harmonic gymnastics with Delsarte. Through him, and through another teacher, Mrs. Richard Hovey, Delsarte's methods became known in America to Isadora Duncan, Ruth St. Denis, and Ted Shawn—a formidably important trio with tremendously wide influence. And in Europe another pupil of Delsarte's passed on the system to Rudolf von Laban, the great Hungarian-born reformer of stage movement. Through him it reached Mary Wigman and the

93

Fred Farren as Dr. Coppélius in *Coppélia,* England, 1906

Adeline Genée as Swanilda and Dorothy Craske as Franz in
Coppélia, England, 1906

Central European Dance. In this way the nonclassical dance schools of America and Europe owe a tremendous debt to Delsarte, whose teaching helped them formulate methods of communication through mime gesture and movement gesture. It is all the more surprising to realize how little his name means to classical ballet enthusiasts.

In the latter half of the nineteenth century a confusing additional meaning for the word "pantomime" crept in. Mime and pantomime are frequently synonymous; in spite of describing different genres in the ancient world, the passing years have brought them into a very close union. But there is one very specialized use of pantomime—the English pantomime.

This curious national tradition, associated mainly with the Christmas season, grew out of the Harlequin plays but got far away from them. It became an entertainment, loosely based on some popular fairy tale, in which singing, dancing, spoken acting, slapstick clowning (the whitewash or custard pie scenes), topical gags, and spectacle were far more in evidence than mime. It was an entertainment in which there was an echo of the old revelry presided over in the Middle Ages by the Lord of Misrule, when everything was topsy-turvy—the servant became the master, the master the servant, and men and women exchanged their clothes and roles. In the English pantomime, Prince Charming was played by a stalwart young woman called the Principal Boy, and the chief comedy character was a Dame played by a man.

But English pantomimes have little to do with pantomime in its sense of mime, except that they usually included, in their heyday, a harlequinade, in which the old commedia dell'arte characters danced and mimed their way through some typical episode.

There was a slight English pantomime flavor to some of the ballets given at the Alhambra and Empire theaters in London at this time, but as far as mime went, they were not to be despised, and one of the most charming stars of this era, the Danish ballerina Adeline Genée, was very much a mistress of comedy mime. When she went on tour in the United States in a show called *The Soul Kiss*, she had headlines such as "The Gamut of human Emotions depicted without one spoken Word." In London, Max Beerbohm wrote of her: "Her dancing . . . is a part of her acting. And her acting, moreover, is of so fine a quality that she makes the old ineloquent conventions of gesture tell their meaning to me, and tell them so exquisitely that I quite forget my craving for words."

The Funambules mime tradition in France continued after Deburau's death. Other Pierrots, less celebrated, followed him, and a new theater, the Folies Nouvelles, succeeded the Funambules. In 1890 a woman played Pierrot for the first time, and successfully.

She was Jane May, and she acted in a play without words, called *L'Enfant Prodigue*, which is still widely quoted as a mime classic. It made such a hit, in London, as well as in Paris, that it is occasionally revived—the most recent production was in London in 1950. It was written first as a play *with* words by Michel Carré, and the words were set to music by Wormser; then mime was substituted for the words, and the play was staged. In it, the story of the prodigal son is given a contemporary (1890) setting, but with the prodigal dressed as Pierrot. The story is simple, straightforward, and a little melodramatic, rather like those of the early silent films.

When it was given in London originally, Jane May was

Jane May in *L'Enfant Prodigue*, 1891

Jane May and Francesca Zanfretta in *L'Enfant Prodigue,*
1891

again Pierrot, Francesca Zanfretta was Phrynetta, and a mime known as Papa Courtes was Pierrot's father. Courtes is quoted as having mimed an account of an accident and death as if he were reading aloud from a newspaper—facial expression, mime gesture—and it was "superb and clear as any speech."

Jane May had begun her mime studies only two years before, when two brothers called Larcher started a Cercle Funambulisque in Paris to revive the traditional Italian pantomime, but in an interview in the *Illustrated London News* she pointed out that there were differences between the commedia dell'arte and the technique used in *L'Enfant Prodigue*. The commedia dell'arte had what she termed a "gesticulative dictionary," which was known and understood by their audiences, whereas the actors in these French mime plays (because *L'Enfant Prodigue* was only one item in their repertoire) used gestures and actions intelligible to any audience. They spoke their parts until nearly the end of the rehearsals, and unlike the commedia dell'arte, there was no impromptu "gagging" in performance. Jane May stressed the need for musical accompaniment to mime (and this is interesting because some schools of thought nowadays feel that it should never be set to music) and also that it was infinitely more exhausting and demanding than spoken acting: "The mental and physical fatigue is tremendous. At the end of a performance I feel absolutely tired out, body and soul."

Zanfretta, an Italian dancer, lived to have a direct influence on the teaching of mime in the Royal Ballet. Ninette de Valois has written about her in *Come Dance with Me,* picturing her in 1928 as an old lady, vigorous, with wonderful style: "Her mime was perfection itself. She taught my head teacher, Ursula Moreton, about two hundred gestures, with every detail of footwork and transfer of weight. Her views on modern mime, when expressed, seemed in danger of giving her a stroke. . . ."

At the turn of the century, mime was flourishing in Paris. Georges Wague was an important figure, holding the post of Professor of Mime at the Paris Opéra and the Opéra-Comique, and mimes were given at various theaters. An unexpected success among the leading ladies was the famous courtesan La Belle Otero, who proved much better at mime than she had ever been at the Spanish dancing which launched her into the theater. The great Pierrot of the day was Severin, but as Europe came up to World War I, tremendous changes were taking place in all the theatrical arts.

Changes in mime were to come mainly from Russia and from inside the classical ballet. Chief of the innovators was the great Michel Fokine. A product of the Imperial Ballet in St. Petersburg, he envisaged ballet in vastly different terms from the ones then prevailing—the full-length, Petipa-style narrative ballet with its alternation of mime scenes and conventional dance patterns of the *pas seul*, the *pas de deux* with variations for the ballerina and the *premier danseur* and a joint coda, the *pas de trois*, the *pas de quatre*, the various types of ensemble. Fokine believed that ballet could become a more vital and expressive theatrical art if it were freed from its traditional demands, and when he came to do choreography, first for the Imperial Ballet and then, so fruitfully, for the Diaghilev Ballet, he worked with five ideals in mind: The type of dancing used in a ballet should be appropriate to the period and the type of theme; dance and mime should express the theme and not be "mere visual entertainment"; gesture should be a matter of the whole body (conventional hand gestures should be used only when the style of work demanded them); the whole choreographic design should be expressive; the choreographer should be free to use any type of music and costume he wished. As far as mime was concerned, Fokine emphasized silent acting and expressive movement and largely discarded the convention of scenes of gesture conversation.

He continued to use significant gesture where necessary. For instance, in his great ballet *Petrushka* about the Russian puppet with the human emotions, all the old gestures for love and hate and fear have their place, but they are used very differently. There are no set dances without meaning, and the story is carried forward by the type of mime which conveys meaning by expressive movements of the whole body. Characters in Fokine's ballets (apart from the pure dance ballets, like the one most familiar to us these days, *Les Sylphides*) are seen in the round, like characters in a play, even the minor ones.

This encouraged great performances from his dancers, and for him, Tamara Karsavina, Vaslav Nijinsky, and Adolph Bolm produced unforgettable characterizations. They also carried forward with great effect the tradition of the Romantic *ballet d'action* with their performances in *Giselle*, and expressive mime was one of the qualities characteristic of Anna Pavlova's genius—that genius whose influence has been so much more widespread—almost incalculable—than that of any other single artist in dance history. The capacity of the great dancer-mimes is often underestimated. They remain in ballet, where dancing is preeminently the admired art, and it is rarely realized that out of ballet they would be capable of brilliant performances as solo pantomime artists. In the same way, the dance dramas of Western classical ballet suffer from being compared with pure dance ballets.

There is really no reason why separate repertoires should not exist, as so frequently is the case in the East.

Fokine's *Carnaval* had paid tribute to the commedia dell'arte and had shown too how fresh the old gesture language could seem when handled in his individual way. The scene between Columbine and Harlequin, when he pretends to wrench his heart from his breast and lay it at her feet, is charming and tender. In comedy mime, however, Fokine was outdone by the next great choreographer to emerge, Leonide Massine. In witty, sparkling ballets such as *La Boutique Fantasque* or *Gaîté Parisienne*, he employed a personal style where mime was fully incorporated into the dance movement, basically linked to the commedia dell'arte but beautifully updated. The can-can dancers of *Boutique*, the Peruvian and the gloveseller of *Gaîté*, and even the miller and his wife in *The Three-Cornered Hat*, are direct descendants of Harlequin and Columbine translated into classical ballet terms of their period.

By the twentieth century we can see two wide categories into which mime has become divided. Out of man's primitive mimes and dance dramas, various sophisticated theatrical styles have proceeded. First, there is the pantomime tradition derived from Greece and Rome and continued through the commedia dell'arte. This has branched into the gesture language and silent acting in classical ballet and in plays and operas, the different forms of gesture and acting of the various European pantomime schools, the clowning of music hall and circus, and the comedy or tragedy of silent films. Second, there are the indigenous dance dramas of countries outside Europe, uninfluenced by Rome and the commedia dell'arte. These range from the complex theaters of Japan, China, and India to many largely less developed or pre-

Tamara Karsavina as Columbine in *Carnaval*

served styles in Negro, American Indian, Middle Eastern, or Australasian tradition.

What has happened to mime *in* the twentieth century? Although the vogue for Pierrot and the mime plays had died down in Paris by World War I, the art of mime still fascinated theater people. From time to time various theatrical directors of genius have seen its possibilities in their stage productions—directors of the caliber of Max Reinhardt, Stanislavsky, Komisarjevsky—and one of these, Copeau, who opened the Théâtre du Vieux-Colombier in 1913, provided a training school for his actors at which pantomime was one of the studies. The plays produced at the Vieux-Colombier (and later by its derivative, the Compagnie des Quinze) pressed mime into the service of "total theater."

One of the students, however, Étienne Decroux, admired the idea of pure pantomime. He revived and built on the lapsed traditions of Deburau and his successors, founding the Théâtre de Mime Français, and his students included Jean-Louis Barrault and Marcel Marceau—a notable record.

Barrault has now turned his great mimetic talent mainly to the use of the spoken theater, starting the Compagnie Madeleine Renaud–Jean-Louis Barrault at the Marigny Theatre in 1946. He has, however, produced four mime plays there; the first, *Baptiste*, originated from the film *Les Enfants du Paradis* in which Barrault played Deburau and staged a scene such as Deburau might have taken part in.

The Harlequin of that scene was Marcel Marceau. In 1947, he started a mime company of his own and has done more than anyone to make French pantomime familiar around the world today. His white-faced Bip, with his flexible body, beautiful hands, and great range of expression stays strictly within the conventions of his medium. As a solo artist, his impressions of life and character move from one extreme to

Marcel Marceau playing the violin

another. Some are purely funny, like the one called *Bip dans une soirée mondaine* ("Bip at a Society Party"), with its silent conversations with invisible people, sometimes leaning on an invisible mantelpiece, its eating embarrassments, and its gaily drunken ending. Some are bitterly satirical, like the vivid portrayals of the glutton or the envious sculptor in his "Seven Deadly Sins." And one or two are intense in feeling, such as the one where the maskmaker tries on a smiling mask and finds he can't get it off. Body and hands show his growing panic and despair, while the face (which expresses the mask) continues to smile contentedly.

Now and then Marceau collects a company, and that is even more interesting. Now and then he makes a film, such as *In the Park* or *The Overcoat*. Because he has traveled so much, he is without doubt the most widely known pantomimist in all the long history of the art.

The cinema has revealed another great French mime of our time—Jacques Tati. Tati began his career in the music hall, with highly successful and amusing mimes on sport. The first film in which he appeared, *Jour de Fête*, proved popular, and since then he has become world famous with *M. Hulot's Holiday* and *Mon Oncle*. The wordless character he plays is a worthy successor to Chaplin and Keaton, an eloquent, if silent, commentator on modern life and habits and as endearing as either Charlie or the Great Stone Face.

Other strands have to be woven into the tapestry. France and Denmark, as we have seen, had the good fortune to have continuing histories of pantomime. Even though in France it sometimes gained and sometimes lost popularity, it never became completely lost itself. Central Europe's tradition, which derives from the medieval morality plays, as

Jacques Tati in *Jour de Fête*

well as from the commedia dell'arte, reached a peak earlier this century, mainly as a result of the widespread enthusiasm for Delsarte's teaching and principles. His influence, partly disseminated through Rudolf von Laban, on such artists of the dance as Mary Wigman and Harald Kreutzberg, who launched the solo pantomime, gave an impetus to the study of mime, and many of Laban's ideas inspired and were developed by Kurt Jooss when he began to choreograph ballets. Jooss believed in a dramatic dance which would combine pure dance and pantomime—not, as we have seen from the eighteenth-century reformers and from Fokine, an unprecedented belief. He spoke of traditional ballet gesture as "like a deaf and dumb language" and aimed at making all meaning explicit in movement and action. In this way he refined the tendency that Central European mime had (and still has, with certain artists) toward the horrific, the grotesque, and the caricature and considerably influenced choreographers both outside and inside classical ballet.

The history of pure pantomime has never been very positive in England. *L'Enfant Prodigue* had its success back in 1891, and it was the inspiration for another Pierrot play, in 1916, *Et Puis Bonsoir*, in which Irene Mawer made her debut. She was probably the most important force for English mime between the world wars. She revived and played in *L'Enfant Prodigue* in 1928, published a classic book *The Art of Mime* in 1932, and founded an Institute of Mime in London in 1933. Since then others, including Harold Cheshire, Ernest Berk, and Lindsay Kemp, have tried to popularize mime by starting schools and companies, but it seems essentially a non-English art—except, of course, in classical ballet.

There mime has found its flowering, as far as England is

City Center Joffrey Ballet in *The Green Table*

concerned. The English dramatic ballet tradition is something of which the English can be proud. Many of the historic works in the repertoires of the Royal Ballet or the Ballet Rambert were outstanding dance dramas, and they encouraged the development of a group of notably excellent mimes. The swing of the 1950's and 1960's has been antinarrative and therefore antidance drama, and dance dramas in terms of classical ballet are not very much in favor; when they are created at all, they seem to be scenes out of a psychiatrist's casebook. In the 1930's and 1940's, however, dramatic ballets of the quality of Ninette de Valois' *The Rake's Progress*, Robert Helpmann's *Miracle in the Gorbals*, Antony Tudor's *Lilac Garden*, Andrée Howard's *Lady into Fox*, or Walter Gore's *The Fugitive* provided tremendous opportunities for creative acting and helped give English ballet and English dancers their great reputation.

The vogue is over for the moment, but artistic climates change. No one would have thought, in the 1940's, that public taste would ever welcome new full-length ballets. Their day seemed over—but with *Ondine, Romeo and Juliet,* and the revised *Fille mal Gardée,* all great popular successes, this has become a laughable idea. So there is always a possibility of a renaissance of the dramatic ballet.

In the United States the beginnings of mime outside ballet are difficult to trace—perhaps they lie with Delsarte and Steele MacKaye and with the enthusiastic love of the Orient which seized Ruth St. Denis in 1904 and led her to study Hindu and Japanese theater. Strong influences came from the silent films—the work of Chaplin, Keaton, and the other great mimes. Then, in the 1930's, various Central European dance and mime recitalists toured the States: Harald Kreutzberg, the Sakharoffs, Alexander von Swaine.

Two of the most notable artists to be fascinated by the art

were Angna Enters and Charles Weidman, who became important names in the history of American mime. Angna Enters, a New Yorker, began performing in 1928 and received Guggenheim fellowships in 1934 and 1935 to study dance and mime in Greece and Egypt. Her program, *Pagan Greece,* in 1938 inaugurated theatrical performances in the Metropolitan Museum; she has toured widely as a mime and recently published a book, *On Mime.* Her view is that mime is a progression of movement and pauses in time rhythms and that, above all, it must have clarity in the expression of its images and under- rather than overstatement in the way it is presented.

Weidman almost entirely excludes facial expression from his ideal of mime, believing that everything can be expressed by the body. He has worked toward the ideal of the Sakharoffs, of "abstract mime." This is an interesting but rather obscure progress. Just as *L'Enfant Prodigue* took a written play and then discarded the words in favor of mime, so Weidman takes a mimed situation and discards its realistic interpretation. He has quoted an example in an essay in *The Dance Has Many Faces:* a musician who has a bucket of water thrown over him, the scene interpreted without implying the character of the musician or indicating any bucket of water. These mimes he terms "kinetic pantomimes."

Classical ballet mime in the United States has been to some extent devalued by the preponderance of nonnarrative ballets deriving from George Balanchine's influence. He himself has used mime on occasion, in *Don Quixote* or *A Midsummer Night's Dream,* as well as in the old shorter works, such as *Night Shadow* or *Prodigal Son. The Nutcracker,* which he rechoreographed in 1954 for the New York City Ballet and which is the great popular Christmas show in New York, has of course plenty of traditional mime in its

Charles Weidman in *Pantomime* from *Suite Intriga*

first act for the children and their parents and, especially, for Drosselmayer. But these works are not in his most typical vein. The native talent in the United States, however, which was excited and encouraged by Pavlova's tours during and after World War I, tended much more to the dramatic or comedy-dramatic ballet. In the 1930's, works by Ruth Page, Catherine Littlefield, Lew Christensen, and Eugene Loring were successful in this style, and it is perhaps a pity that this has been largely forgotten. In the 1940's the Ballet Theater repertoire produced a good many story ballets, notably by Agnes De Mille. Antony Tudor was recruited from England, and his dramatic ballets *Pillar of Fire, Romeo and Juliet,* and *The Lady of the Camellias* developed the style that marks his earlier works, like *Lilac Garden*—psychological characterization shown by expressive mime. These choreographers served fine dancer-mimes, such as Nora Kaye (the sensitive, suffering Hagar of *Pillar of Fire*), Muriel Bentley, and Hugh Laing.

Outside classical ballet, Martha Graham and José Limon have their own moods and expressive conventions. Limon, a Mexican, has based dramatic ballets on national themes (*La Malinche*) and on Shakespeare (*The Moor's Pavane*). Graham began her studies at Denishawn, the Ruth St. Denis and Ted Shawn School of Dancing and Related Art, and there, of course, came in contact with the ideas of Delsarte, but her methods in creating dance dramas are strikingly individual and have been developed over the years. In many of them, particularly the most recent, the dramatic impact comes entirely from the combination of expressive dance movement, music, and inspired decor, but silent acting has its place in her striking Greek creations, such as *Clytemnestra.* Development of character and situation, rather than

Martha Graham in *Clytemnestra*

narrative mime, is what characterizes a ballet of the Graham school.

A few solo pantomimists are making some impact on the U.S. scene. There is Lionel Shepard, who brings a topical, satirical touch to his work, and Bernard Bragg, who, apart from his work with the National Theater of the Deaf, has televised a series as the Quiet Man. There is Adam Darius, who became inspired with the idea of mime after seeing *Les Enfants du Paradis* and has established himself internationally in one-man shows and working with small companies.

The Middle Eastern countries have not yielded mime traditions to any large extent, apart from the use of mime and mimicry by that very important character of the Semitic races, the storyteller. Small companies have existed, however, even if they have not been widely known; one of the few to be chronicled was in existence just before World War I. It was an all-male, twelve-person troupe, celebrated for its mimes of village and harem life and for its mimicries of birds and animals. Its leader and star was a native of Cairo, Ahmed Fahim al-Far ("the Mouse"), and it probably had counterparts in other places and at other periods. Dance pantomimes have always been known in Iran. A good many of them, as in Roman and Greek days, were daring and indecent, but others were in the nature of comic ballets or interpretations of poetry or song. Hebrew dance dramas can be seen in the repertoire of the Yemenite Jewish company, Inbal, and mime plays its part in the work of the Habima and elsewhere in the Israeli theatrical scene. Adam Darius has worked in both Tel Aviv and Haifa, and during his time in Israel taught both mime and dancing in the Arab-Jewish Cultural Center in Haifa.

Although the Negro theater, whether in America or in Africa, has never evolved any complicated gesture language, mime in the sense of expressive acting is highly developed. Dance companies from African territories—Guinea, Senegal, Nigeria, and so on—have toured overseas, and their repertoires have included dance dramas about village life, jealousy and love, witchcraft, and violence. A typical one, from the repertoire of the African Ballet of Guinea, founded in 1947, is called *The Forest*. It is a melodramatic tale of how a girl is enticed into the forest and seduced, and because of this outrage to the tribal morals, the vengeful spirits of dead ancestors appear to her and terrorize her, so that she dies of remorse and fear. The whole effect of the ballet depends on the ability of the girl to convey, by facial expression and physical movement, the betrayal of innocence and the horror with which she is possessed when confronted by the terrible apparitions; the fact that it becomes hauntingly memorable is proof of the interpreter's skill in mime. Comic mime is equally well handled. The Senegal Ballet's production *Sindiely* is a marital comedy in which character is everything and the parts of a greedy father, his self-willed daughter, her true love, and the rich man her father tries to marry her to are played with the expert understanding and relish of true comedians.

Negro dancers have such a strong ability for silent acting that on a highly sophisticated level the work of such artists as Mary Hinkson, William Louther, and Dudley Williams is as effective and moving as anything one can see in the dance theater today. They understand the secret of this kind of mime, which is that technique should be completely mastered by and subservient to sincere conviction and feeling for character and situation.

Negro and American Indian dance come together in the

The Forest (African Ballet of Guinea)

Caribbean and have been given fame through the work of Katherine Dunham. There, as in the Philippines, various European influences (Spanish, Dutch, French, and English) have also been felt. Amerindian cultures in North, Central, and South America were once rich in dance drama. Tribes passed on their history from one generation to another by dramatic dance and pantomime to the accompaniment of song. This custom seemed politically dangerous to their European conquerors, and it was ruthlessly stamped out, so that only some dances of mimicry or dances without direct dramatic significance survived. The thread was deliberately and wantonly broken, and now, when a more liberal attitude and an interest in cultural traditions have prevailed, it is proving difficult to resurrect these dramatic arts, even though valiant attempts are being made.

The work of the twentieth century, then, has been to continue the old mime traditions, but even more important, outside Europe it has revived or revivified many dead or dying theater arts. As countries and peoples have gained independence, they have tended to promote their national cultures, and the dance drama companies in Africa, for instance, are examples of this. In India an active preservation campaign was waged a number of years ago and has resulted in a great strengthening of its magnificent traditions. The Chinese classical theater has survived political changes (and indeed split itself into two, for there is a Chinese classical theater in Formosa, as well as in Peking); the Japanese *nō* and kabuki continue in unabated popularity. New interest in old cultures has been shown in the Central and South American countries.

All forms of gesture and silent acting, however, widely different though they may be in technique or cultural background, still have exactly the same intention that marked the hunting story acted out to campfire watchers. They are man's daily experience, his emotions and thoughts, reflected back to him by the faithful mirror of the skilled mime. As long as this identification between artist and audience exists, mime will survive as an important method of theatrical communication.

Part III

AN EXCURSION INTO TECHNIQUE

Now what of the technique and the training for mime? Both are as rigorous as for any form of dance or drama. They have similarities from one century to another or from one country to another, but there are also differences.

The basic skills needed for good mime are the same everywhere: physical suppleness and control, backed by intelligence and human understanding—and of course, complete command of whichever gesture language is used to communicate in the particular school of mime to which the actor belongs. The Roman mime is the first for whom we have qualifications listed. Lucian claimed that he had to have memory, sensibility, shrewdness, rapidity of conception, and tact; that he had to be a good judge of music and poetry and physically well proportioned, as well as strong and supple. He also had to be thoroughly well read in the history and myths known to his audiences. We know relatively nothing of the sort of training he got for all this or the kind of gesture language he had to learn. What we do know from those days is something about social and public gesture, and this is of significance because mime always has a relationship with the gestures of its time. It adopts and uses anything topical and new.

Roman gesture differed a certain amount from our contemporary habits. To say no, you tipped your head back instead of shaking it; instead of clapping the palms of the hands together in applause, you struck the right fist into the left palm. To point at someone was to pay him a compliment. Our gesture of putting out our tongue at someone began in Roman times, however, first as a protection against evil and then—an easy transition—as a calculated insult. Love was indicated by a circle made by the right thumb and forefinger—have you seen this gesture in everyday use at all? It is fairly common among the Latin races, usually accompanied by a little smile and a slight narrowing of the eyes and meaning that somebody or something is absolute perfection!

If the Roman mime had to be supple, shrewd, and mentally quick the comedians of the commedia dell'arte needed a full equipment of these qualities, too, in order to improvise and adapt their plays to suit their audiences. They used spoken dialogue, of course, so that their gestures did not become stylized into a complete language. But when John Rich turned Harlequin into a wordless dance character, significant gestures began to take over.

Rich's Harlequin tradition, which applies to others, like the Danish Pantomimeteater, knew five basic moods: consternation, admiration, agitation, defiance, and determination. Each had its set position for feet, hands, and head. Joan Lawson, in her masterly study for practicing students of mime, gives a nice précis of how these could be used in a scene:

> Harlequin enters to meet Columbine, but expresses *consternation* because she is not at the trysting place. She arrives, he salutes her and expresses *admiration*. But their lovemaking is disturbed and he expresses *agitation*, which turns to *defiance* when the intruder refuses to leave and then to *determination* to fight for his lady.

A good many commedia dell'arte gestures are found in classical ballet mime; scenes and situations, too, echo each other.

The only way we can begin to understand what lay behind any of these famous mimes of the past is to consider the training of present-day mimes. First, the kinds of exercises —breathing exercises, in all positions, followed by exercises to relax and loosen all the muscles of head, neck, trunk, and limbs. Some of these are similar to those for ballet, the various *pliés* (knee bends), for instance. Then there are exercises, based on French pantomime, which help control and suppleness but also link up with working gestures: grasping a pole (imaginary, of course) in various ways, pulling on ropes, holding boxes, moving furniture. There are balancing exercises—some as universally known as walking with a book on the head, that favorite of nineteenth-century governesses to improve the carriage of their young ladies; some as specialized as walking with the arms raised to the side, so that shoulder and elbow are in a straight line but with the forearms hanging down and a book balanced on each upper arm. There are rhythmical exercises, swinging limbs and body; slow-motion exercises, hand and finger exercises; exercises in showing characters and situations in movement. How would you like, for instance, to try dying as differently as Desdemona, Romeo, and Richard III?

There are exercises you can do wearing a mask so that you concentrate on making your body expressive; there are exercises in perspective—such as walking away without moving off one spot, merely by altering the speed and type of movement. Marceau does this and climbs invisible stairs so convincingly that you have a mental picture of them.

An Excursion into Technique

The simplest actions can be done in so many ways. Take walking—you can be asked to walk as an elderly person, a very old person, in tight shoes, in rubber boots on mud, in bare feet on pebbles. All this and the countless other ways of walking by all kinds of people in all kinds of moods and situations need a great development of imagination. Sometimes, perhaps, you almost have to try to do the actual thing —try, for instance, walking in rubber boots on mud—and then analyze how, exactly, your body reacted, to get the correct effect.

And when you remember that walking is only one branch of activity, you begin to realize how extensive are the requirements of even ordinary mimicry or mimicry with feeling added to it, let alone the speaking of sentences in a set gesture language or the silent acting that puts all these technical achievements in their place.

In addition to all the exercises, a mime has to do a great deal of thinking and studying—his subject being people. He has to analyze so that he can use in mime, age, sex, character, feelings, habits, occupations, and periods of history how human beings react to animals or nature or weather, how they use inanimate objects. All the time he has to sharpen his imagination. The teacher is constantly saying, "Imagine yourself (or the character you are creating) wading a stream, coming in out of the snow, smelling fresh bread, tasting something bitter. Imagine—"

This is one of the miracles of mime, both in the player and the viewer—it enlarges the powers of imagination. And imagination, of course, is the force that raises man to his highest level, either by making him create and appreciate poetry or music or painting or by making him sensitive to the needs and reactions of his fellowmen.

Turning to the Oriental schools of dance drama, what kinds of training do *they* involve? If a Western mime works hard and begins early in life, Oriental mimes are even more dedicated. But dedicated is a rather grim word, implying something humorless and serious and stiff, and none of these qualities ever really typifies the mime. All the same, the Chinese classical theater, the Japanese *nō* and kabuki, the Indian dance drama groups, and the Balinese or Thai dance companies are complete taskmasters in a way that the West only approximates. The players start when they are very young children—anywhere between five and eight years old —and some of them have to train not only their bodies to be immensely flexible; but also their voices since they may be called on to speak or sing. In China or Japan certain passages in the dramas are vocal, just as others are entirely gesture or movement. Probably no forms of theater are more completely disciplined than these of the East and of India. Variations of action or gesture are hardly permitted; there are no bright individual alterations to the characterizations —how different from those informal commedia dell'arte performances which relied on impromptu scenes and action and what actors (as well as jazz musicians) term ad-libbing— inventing as you go along.

In India, dancers aim at the peak of physical flexibility. More than Western dancers they take advantage of the daily services of masseurs, who oil and massage their bodies, and this, combined with their exercises, means that face and neck, body and limbs, as a whole or in their several parts, become perfect instruments for the movements and gestures they have to perform. Students rise early and spend hours on their training, doing eye exercises, for instance, until the eyes are strained and bloodshot, and in the intervals of physical training they learn from their guru (their teacher) all the classic stories in their great Sanskrit books, the *Rāmā-yana* and *Mahābhārata,* so that they know the characters and legends far more thoroughly than English-speaking children know the Greek myths and epics. The guru, in fact, becomes the arbiter of their whole lives, accepting service and homage in return for the knowledge he passes on to them. Stamina, which Western teachers rightly talk of as an essential for both dancers and mime, is even more necessary in the East, because performances continue for many hours, constituting a great physical and emotional strain. Entertainments in Burma, for example, start about nine in the evening and end about four o'clock next morning, and while the audience behaves like most Oriental audiences, treating it as an informally relaxing social occasion, punctuated by refreshments and private talk and only at certain points commanding their whole attention, the actors have to concentrate on every part of the work.

Hand exercises in the East are very different in type and intention from those of the West. They are aimed at complete flexibility. Watching dancers from India or Thailand or Burma, one is impressed and fascinated by the hand and finger movements. Many of them recall figures in Oriental sculpture, which stand in apparently impossible positions, and it is a revelation to realize that human beings can look just like that, given specialized training. Fingers are bent back diligently, separately and together; hands are placed palm to palm and raised at right angles to the arms; gradually it becomes possible for the fingers to bend back without deliberate pressure.

Other exercises make the elbows, the knees, hips, and feet equally flexible in what seem to us completely unnatural ways, and because all these are done steadily and perseveringly from early childhood, they become second nature to the dancer and can be taken for granted by the viewer. They do, however, extend the sphere in which gestures can be made; obviously, if you can move all your joints inward as well as outward, you can double your silent vocabulary. Flexible bodies, too, can bring the feet more into play, and in one of the many folk theater traditions of India they have a gesture language of their own. This is the masked *Chhau* dance drama of Seraikela in Bihar, and the foot and toe gestures are called *upalayas*.

As we have said, each mime tradition has its own ways of communicating, its own significant gestures. These fall into categories. A player can communicate with an audience by hand gestures, arm gestures, gestures of head and shoulders, and facial expression. The way he makes use of his costume can be significant; his makeup or, at certain periods and in certain countries, his mask can convey additional points of information.

Western ballet uses many types of physical gesture. In Part I, when we were talking about *Giselle* and *Coppélia*, we spoke of a few gestures, but there are many more. Usually they are interrelated. As we saw with the gesture for sorrow, the hands suggested flowing tears, shoulders and head dropped forward, the eyes were downcast; for dancing, everything was reversed—the arms were raised, the hands twisted on high, the head and shoulders were flung back, the eyes looked up. As classical ballet is based on five positions of the feet, of the arms, and of the head, so classical ballet mime is also built on this basis; every gesture is developed from these traditional positions. It is worth remembering, too, because of their relevance to classical mime, the seven movements of the classical dance: *plier* (to bend), *étendre* (to stretch), *relever* (to rise), *glisser* (to glide),

An Excursion into Technique

sauter (to jump), *élancer* (to dart), and *tourner* (to turn). It is easy to see how gestures are linked with these categories.

Because of this close connection between classical mime and dance, a gesture in classical ballet can be expressed in dance terms. The gesture for dance, in dance terms, would go like this:

> Arms raised to low *demi-seconde* (that means not quite halfway up to the second position of the arms); then through preparatory and first to third position, keeping one hand slightly below the other in the third position; circle the hands once round each other, then open and lower the arms through the second position.

Some classical ballet gestures have very distant origins—they can be seen on friezes and vase paintings of ancient Greece; some have descended from Roman mime by way of the commedia dell'arte; some have crept in from other sources or from the religious or social gestures of everyday life. But they all have been translated into the terms of the technique of classical ballet.

Greek sculpture and ceramics are the basis, apparently, for the type of gesture used in operetta. There the heroine often accompanies her singing or speech with arm movements reminiscent of a Greek statue. Her arm will be raised in a natural position, a softly curving line from shoulder to wrist, and then the hand will be tilted slightly up and forward. When she points, the same position serves except that she uses the forefinger to do so and droops the other fingers toward the thumb. She has four levels for pointing—floor level (which goes with a command), waist level (which she probably uses for pointing to people or things near her, or inward to herself), shoulder level (for greater distance), and above her head (which becomes a solemn affirmation or protestation). The arm above the head, without pointing, is a greeting or salute or a farewell. She may not, in fact, study or work all this out so analytically and may simply instinctively follow what earlier operetta singers have done; but I think you'll catch her at some, if not all, of these gestures. Otherwise, characters in operetta use familiar basic gestures, and one rule they have to observe, consciously or unconsciously, is to time each gesture so that it emphasizes the sung or spoken word it applies to and is held long enough to form a link with the reaction or reply.

Hand gestures are very important in Chinese dance drama. Six types are differentiated. There is the open hand, varied slightly according to the sex and age of the character represented; this gesture immediately tells an aware audience whether the role is that of an old man, a young man, or a woman. There is the pointing hand—which is just what it sounds like. There is the helpless hand, where the hands are extended limply, palms upward (this is accompanied by a shake of the head). If you try this one, you'll find that it is the very essence of helplessness. There is the hindering hand, which can also mean a refusal—and this is very like the gesture we saw in Act I of *Coppélia*, when Swanilda ended her appeal to Coppélia to come and talk to her: hands raised, palms outward to one side, the head turned in the opposite direction. There is the yielding hand, a more complicated circling movement, which also indicates sorrow or disappointment. Last, there is the contemplative hand. This has one or two alternatives, and one is very like the classical ballet gesture "to think." The Chinese place the middle finger of the left hand against the temple and drop the head, eyes lowered. In classical ballet it can be done with either hand, and the middle finger touches the side of the brow twice.

Six types of hand gesture are modest in number compared with the *hasta mudra* of the Hindu dance. There are a great many of these, although they all come into one of two broad categories: single hand or double hand. Some analyses mention thirty-one single-hand gestures and twenty-seven double-hand gestures, but their permutations and combinations run into the hundreds. Their meaning can often be either realistic or symbolic; the beautiful one meaning a lotus flower, for instance, where the hands are raised, wrist to wrist, with the fingers forming a cup, is also symbolic of love. Head movements (twenty-four are listed) include shaking, rolling, tossing, turning, while twenty-six glances and six eyebrow movements show the care with which every section of physical movement is analyzed.

Japanese *nō* theater has its own rigidly set hand gestures and other movements which illustrate the text of each play, and both *nō* and kabuki possess a fan language which has great beauty, as well as meaning. A closed fan, pointed at someone, is an insult; raised on high, it shows triumph; the dancer traces outlines of mountains with it, opens it, fluttering, to indicate wind, or uses it as a weapon. Its many significant movements make it a very eloquent stage property.

The khon and lakhon of Thailand both depend largely on hand gestures: masks in the khon tradition and made-up poker faces in lakhon mean that nothing can be conveyed by facial expression. The hand gestures are unlike those of other countries, although they have kinship with the conventions of India or Ceylon. For sorrow, where in classical ballet you indicate tears coursing down the cheeks, the Thai dancer wipes away invisible tears with the left hand; for anger, where in classical ballet you raise clenched hands and shake the fists, the Thai dancer points with one forefinger while she stamps her foot; for laughter, you can, in classical ballet, merely laugh soundlessly, but the Thai dancer has to outline a smiling mouth with her two forefingers on lips that never change position.

Cambodian dancers have gestures as linked to those of Thailand as French, Italian, and Spanish are linked as languages. The same root (a Latin one) gives us, say, *la nuit, la notte* and *la noche*—and so a Cambodian dancer will, for instance, outline the smiling mouth as a Thai dancer does but with the joined thumb and forefinger of one hand instead of the two forefingers.

The amount of analysis possible in breaking down the various emotions so that they can be properly distinguished by mime is evidenced by an illustration from the Chinese theater. The Chinese divide laughter into almost twenty categories. When you begin to think of it, of course, this is quite possible. They begin their list with happy laughter and go on to conceited laughter, flattering laughter, uneasy laughter, insane laughter. Every feeling and reaction, obviously, can be subdivided like this, and it is the mime's business to discover how he can best express the variations so that his particular audience can understand and appreciate them.

The Chinese theater has another type of gesture language —sleeve movement. A long cuff of white silk, between one and two feet long, is sewn into the sleeve of the costume and left open at the seam, and the player learns various ways of using this significantly. About fifty ways exist. Whenever an actor comes onstage, he uses a turning sleeve movement which indicates that the orchestra should start, and the way he does this is watched eagerly by the audience. If they are connoisseurs of sleeve movement, they can gauge his skill by this preliminary gesture. To introduce the scene, he faces slightly right, raises his left hand to chin level, and holds the lower corner of the left sleeve with his right hand. To show embarrassment or suggest invisibility, the sleeve is held before his face. This is termed the concealing sleeve, and allied to it is the aside sleeve—a similar gesture, but not hiding the face so much. This position, if you imagine it without the sleeve, is very like the one characters in old-fashioned melodramas used to adopt for their spoken asides, which were intended for the audience but not supposed to be heard by the other people onstage.

Then there is the repulsing sleeve, which has a couple of variations. The most dramatic is where you make a circle with your hand and then move your arm so that your sleeve flies out in a violent way in the direction of the other character. For the weeping sleeve you use the tip of the sleeve to dab at invisible tears. The resting sleeve shows despair or possibly that the character is meant to be a ghost; the arms hang down limply by the sides. When you take a big decision, you stretch out the right arm, twist your hand inward and then outward, and then drop it from the wrist with the palm to the audience; this is the resolution sleeve. In excitement or anger, you move an arm inward and outward quickly and catch up the tip of the same sleeve as you do it. The management of these sleeves is an art in which some players excel more than others.

Closely akin to the sleeve gestures are movements of the marvelous pheasant-tail headdresses some of the players wear. Generals—many Chinese stories feature generals—hold them with the tips of their fingers and at a higher level than ordinary old men; women hold them just above the shoulders. A tremendously effective gesture is the one showing anger, called winding the feathers, when you move your head so that the feathers sweep a great circle. For surprise or sometimes for contemplation you dip your head so that the feathers tip over and touch the floor. The firmest determination is shown by holding the tips of the feathers between your teeth.

A multitude of charming conventional movements come into Chinese plays, as well as into opera or dance. To enter a house, the player steps over an invisible high threshold (evil spirits cannot get over a raised barrier, so Chinese houses used to be built that way); to do it, he picks up his robe slightly and raises his foot with a slight circling movement. To indicate riding, he mimes mounting a horse; then pulling on the reins with the left hand and holding a whip (a real whip, with tassels on it) high in the right hand, he moves off at a trot. Various types of balancing represent various activities—rowing a boat, climbing a hill, swimming, slipping on mud.

A perfect mime episode in the Chinese style is described in *Chinese Theater* by Kalvodova-sis-vanis. It is about a maid who is asked by her mistress to pick a particular flower off a blossoming tree. She brings on an invisible ladder, with an effort props it against the tree, and anchors it with a stone against one of its uprights. She climbs, sways slightly at the top, reaches out to the flower, withdraws her hand with a look of annoyance as she sees a wasp on it; then she pauses, watches the wasp fly off, picks the flower. Now, with the flower in her right hand and the top of the ladder in her left, she is bothered by a fly settling on her brow. She looks up at it, then blows upward to dislodge it. She then puts the flower in her hair and, using both hands, climbs down the ladder.

This has affinities with Marcel Marceau's billposter—carrying the ladder, climbing it, and so on. The techniques are not unlike, but there is a subtle difference in the intention and the attitude of the player. The Chinese episode is part of a play, and the player interprets it as an actor would. The French episode is an item on its own, an isolated piece of observed action which, because of its isolation, is more artificial than the Chinese one. The difference *is* a subtle one—but where the French episode leads one to say, "How lifelike, how amusing, what a cleverly observed reflection of something we might see any day," the Chinese one, taken for granted in the context of a story, seems more natural and unexaggerated. One admires the French item but accepts the Chinese as one would accept a comedy scene in a straight play.

Eastern mime and, of course, primitive mime devote as much painstaking skill to the imitation of animals and birds as they do to human beings. The Western mime neglects this side of his art almost entirely. This is probably because the animal world, both in its appeal to the hunter and in its significance in religious legend, is of vital importance to the Oriental mind; whatever the reason, the fact remains that the natural history element in mime features little in the West.

Animal pantomime is as old as the caveman's campfire, but it also forms a very sophisticated form of mime in most Eastern traditions. African and American Indian dances or Australian corroborees all yield their brilliant mimicries of local wildlife, but the religious and classic dance dramas of the East have important episodes dealing with animal characters. Many of the scenes involve descriptions of forests teeming with animal life, of rivers full of fish, of flocks of birds. A kathakali dancer in the role of an ancient prince will, like our own Prince Siegfried, go out hunting, but whereas Siegfried will merely arm himself with a crossbow and walk around while the backdrop changes to that of the swan lake, the kathakali prince will, by set gestures, tell us about the forest and what he sees there. He will describe trees, with twisting upward movements of the hands; his arms stretch out like branches, and the hands form leaves and flowers. He will describe a lion, a panther, an elephant, a group of chattering monkeys, a bounding deer; he will show us birds in the air and fish in the stream. A Burmese dancer, instead of using the conventional, although vividly descriptive, gesture for some animal as does a kathakali dancer, introduces a complete mimicry of the creature, its walk and way of feeding, its nature and reactions. And in a fascinating book, *Dance and Drama in Bali,* Beryl de Zoete wrote about the movements and gestures of animals that the dancers there represent:

> The slow rocking hops and curious pushing steps accompanied by quick circling glances of the lions; the wide springs, with two feet together, of the birds; the little zigzagging steps and high rising on toes, with a sigh, the coy twisting springs and furtive gestures of the deer; the curvetting step and rearing neck of the snake and the dipping roll of the elephant.

Most important of all are the monkey people. This is mainly because one of the most lovable and beloved of legendary characters in the East is the monkey god, Hanuman. There is a book, translated into English by Arthur Waley under the title *Monkey,* which deals with Hanuman's adventures and magic powers, and a good many of the dance dramas in India, China, and Indonesia take him as their hero. In consequence, the technique of playing monkeys in the various grades—ordinary monkeys, royal monkeys (like the rival princes of the *Rāmāyana*), and Hanuman himself— is very fully developed. Birds, too, are brilliantly observed, in swooping, flying, and feather-ruffling movements.

Of course Western choreographers have not entirely overlooked the possibilities of animal and bird mimicry. Admittedly there is little in *Swan Lake* reminiscent of swans—except perhaps the slight preening movements of the head against the shoulders that the Swan Queen makes when she first comes out of the lake and the sweeping flight movement of her arms. *The Firebird* has many birdlike movements, whether in Fokine's or Balanchine's choreography. Petipa's White Cat and Puss-in-Boots in *The Sleeping Beauty* sidle and scratch convincingly, and Ashton's rooster and hens in *La Fille mal Gardée* always stir amused recognition in the audience. But the majority of birds, cats, and dogs that adorn the Western ballet stage are superficial in their mimicry and give the distinct impression that the choreographers have no great feeling for their subjects. The main intention is to sketch in the association or, in the humorous ballet, to guy the characteristics—not to portray the creature. Helpmann's lyrebird in *The Display* comes nearer than most to the Oriental mood in its convincing observation and approach, as anyone who has watched the lyrebird's courting dance in the forests of Australia can testify.

A method of communication which lies outside the realm of mime and gesture language and which yet has always been so closely associated with dance drama and pantomime that it must be touched on is by means of makeup and masks. The use of masks is ancient. They had dual purposes—to convey some message to an audience and to impress and excite them. The kind of message they could convey was the character being presented—male, female, young, old, human or superhuman or animal, serious or comic. The emotions they could arouse of wonder or terror came from the beauty or malignity of the expression or the magnificence of the workmanship.

Greek and Roman actors wore masks with open mouths, so that sound could be heard; the mimes' masks had closed mouths, to fit their silent acting. Always where enormous open-air theaters were used, masks played an important part in communicating with the audience; and because they could arouse the same kind of pleasure in spectators as can elaborate decor and costumes, lighting effects or mechanical transformations in the modern theater, there are a vast number of marvelous designs to be found in communities all over the world. All reflect their national art and culture, from the Inca and Aztec masks to those of Europe, Africa, or Asia.

But masks obscure mime, rather than aid it, because mime, as we have seen, includes facial expression, and the best mime can convey all it needs to without artificial aids. Noverre wrote about this, pointing out that masks have "but one permanent and unvarying character" (although some of the Greek and Roman ones, he recalls, were made up of two halves, one sad, one gay; the actor presented whichever side was appropriate to the audience), and he pleaded eloquently for banishing them and relying on "the lively and animated expression" of the artists.

He was in favor of replacing them by imaginative make-up, and makeup, of course, is in a very different category from masks. The talented mime can get his effects brilliantly *without* using makeup—if you can ever find one who will demonstrate this to you, don't miss the chance. You will see him, purely by thought-controlled muscles, range through a wide territory of human types and moods. But makeup can enhance these effects and at the same time incorporate the two purposes of masks without the fixed and static character of masks.

Character makeup was one of the reforms urged by Noverre, and he cited the great actor David Garrick as an example of what could be done in this line. "He knew how to dispose brush strokes on the prominent parts of the face according to the needs of the character he was playing...." Nowadays character makeup is something we expect to be good in both plays and ballets, although even now some artists are better at it than others. But once again the difference between West and East is clear. There is no universal makeup, say, for Coppélius; each dancer invents and depicts his own, which suits his face and the character line he is following. But in India and China elaborate makeup follows traditional designs; the differences—and they do, of course, exist—between appearances lie in the fact that a traditionally designed makeup applied to a human face has a different result in each case. The Japanese *nō* theater uses both masks and makeup—the masks and the angles at which they are presented have significance—but the kabuki mainly relies on makeup. Sometimes, as with the Chinese and the Indian kathakali theaters, this complicated makeup is referred to as a mask, which is misleading; it is in fact built up on the face itself.

The process takes hours—about five, in the case of kathakali. The players use the time as a period of relaxation and meditation, for the main part of the makeup is done for them, while they lie on the ground, by expert makeup men. Instead of using prepared sticks of greasepaint, these makeup men mix their own colors, like artists, in earthenware or coconut-shell pots, and then begin to build up the character type on the face of the actor. Say, for instance, that he is to be a green type—a hero or a god. A clear green paste is used for the base, and a characteristic feature of kathakali makeup, a white framework of rice paste, shaped a little like a small collar, is attached to the face. The points of the collar come at the corner of each eye, and its circle lies down the line of the cheeks and around the upper part of the chin just below the mouth. Firm black lines elongate the eyes and mark the eyebrows, the lips are brightly red, and a stylized design is painted in gold and black on the brow. The other makeup types, the red demons and passionate characters, the gold priests and women, are built up in similar ways to carefully worked-out plans.

The Chinese actor applies his own makeup, with a long reed-handled brush and liquid paint. Most of the designs date back about 500 years. The color significance is at points directly opposed to the kathakali—red faces are heroes, and green are demons; women are pale pink; evil characters are white; supernatural beings are gold. Other colors appear. Black faces are also good, upright characters; blue are courageous and rather wild; yellow are intelligent and scholarly; brown are strong and obstinate people. With the colors, oil or white of egg is mixed, so that the makeup glistens magically in the stage lighting.

The Western theater has very little in the way of fixed traditional makeup. Pierrot has a whitened face, and this convention has been adopted by French pantomime artists, with individual variations of feature: black-rimmed eyes, often with a vertical line centralized above and below, as if the eyes were bisected; arched eyebrows above normal eyebrow level, and downcurved red mouth. Clown is more elaborate and colorful—frequently a white base, arched eyebrows and upturned mouth, with individual variants of brow and cheek design.

An Excursion into Technique

Quite a few conventional makeup ideas appear in the handbooks and continue to be put to use onstage, but no real rules apply. The Western artist has endless scope and freedom—far more, in fact, than he normally avails himself of.

Turning to silent acting in ballet, one finds that dancers can be roughly divided into two categories in their methods of working: those who simply express the choreographer's conception of character, and those who create character themselves. The first group is not to be despised. They learn their interpretation at the knee of the choreographer, who does their creative work for them, but they are highly refined precision instruments by which he can communicate with the audience. Dancers of the other group, however, behave exactly as actors and actresses in the legitimate theater do. They prepare a role by study, thought, discussion, experiment, imagination—and add that final state of being receptive to atmosphere and to the needs of the theater which always raises the pitch of a performance.

There are many great acting roles both in the traditional and in contemporary ballet and many very rewarding minor ones. They make vastly different demands on their interpreters.

In the traditional ballets, as we have seen, the dancer has to act the part and also has to be master of the gesture language by which the mimed scenes convey their meaning. Apart from that, there are differences in style in the music, the choreography, and the subject, particularly whether it is comedy or tragedy. You might think that a dance actress capable of the tragedy of Giselle could equally well play Odette-Odile. This is far from true. Although the same basic equipment is needed—a perfected gesture language technique, an ability to comprehend the character of a woman involved in a tragic love affair, an ability to move the audience to sorrow and pity—the two roles are made sharply different by two elements. These are the music—in one case the tunefully dramatic melodies of Adolphe Adam, and in the other the impassioned lyricism of Tchaikovsky—and the style of choreography—*Giselle*, a romantic ballet heroine, is allowed a more passionate and a freer style of communication than Odette, whose interpretation is severely disciplined.

In more modern dramatic works, you will begin to appreciate the enormous variety of problems confronting the dancer if you think about some of the ballets they may be called on to interpret. There are totally different sorts of tragic statement in Balanchine's *Prodigal Son*, De Mille's *Fall River Legend*, Tudor's *Pillar of Fire*, in Ashton's *Ondine*, MacMillan's *Romeo and Juliet*, De Valois' *The Rake's Progress*. Yet all these are based on classical ballet technique. *Prodigal Son* needs playing of a disciplined, almost stylized quality, in which gesture is used in a formal, although very moving, way. It is a series of images representing the various states of life or experience through which the son passes. He is, in sequence, proud, independent, worldly; humiliated, forsaken, distressed; and, finally, repentant. It is one of the roles where the choreographer has so framed the movements and gestures that the effect can almost be made by the choreography alone without any acting or facial expression from the dancer. In the hands of a fine actor-dancer it can gain in impact, of course, but as long as the choreography is correctly performed, it will be effective.

Fall River Legend, on the other hand, stands or falls by the total conviction and intensity of acting with which the dancer of the woman invests the part. It is a more emotional work than *Prodigal Son,* and it can be more or less of an

Edward Villella in *Prodigal Son* (New York City Ballet)

emotional experience for the audience according to the personal effect made by the leading dancer. *Pillar of Fire,* like all Tudor's work, demands dancers who are capable of making major impressions in minor keys—its great dramatic feeling has to be understated, hinted at, rather than acted all stops out, as *Fall River Legend* should be. It needs a mood of tension and restraint and inhibition—and then by contrast the moments of abandoned feeling blaze up as from a smoldering fire.

Ondine requires immense delicacy of romantic touch in its handling of tragedy, a quality of the sad fairy-tale ballad. *Romeo and Juliet* is strongly lyrical, but also lyrically dramatic; it combines subtle acting for Juliet with heavy drama, as in Tybalt's death. *The Rake's Progress* is a masterpiece of the tragic character ballet which involves every force at a dancer's command—acting, both subtle and fully expressive, characterization over a period of time, mimetic gesture and facial expression, as well as a meticulous understanding of its period (the eighteenth century).

One of the most widely known of recently composed ballets, because it has been filmed, as well as toured extensively, with Fonteyn and Nureyev in the leads, is Kenneth Mac-Millan's *Romeo and Juliet,* and it is an interesting study from the mime point of view. The traditional and the contemporary meet at many points, and both gesture and silent acting are employed at various levels.

Everyone who has studied Shakespeare's play or seen it staged is familiar with the difficulties of acting the part of Juliet. It's a well-worn tag to say that no actress has the experience to play Juliet until she is too old to be convincing as a fourteen-year-old girl—even a mature sixteenth-century Italian of that age. But of course, this partly applies to the difficulties of speaking the part; it needs immense vocal control and variety, as well as all the other qualities. In the ballet, dance technique, of course, takes the place of verse speaking, but a sufficient mastery of dance technique is possible for a dancer at quite an early age. This is partly the reason why not only Fonteyn but the younger dancers who have tackled the role have been able to make it convincing and moving. Each has given it her individual quality, and everyone puts them in different orders of merit according to his individual taste.

At the beginning Juliet appears as little more than a child—younger, really, than she should be; she is still playing with dolls and teasing her nurse. Her acting has to show her mischievous, thoughtless, innocent, youthfully gauche. Her first scene brings her into contact with two of the important completely mimed roles: her mother, Lady Capulet, and the nurse. These two, together with Lord Capulet, the duke, and Friar Laurence, are strongly characterized in a very traditional style. They might have been created in the nineteenth century, for they are close kin to Giselle's mother, to Bathilde, and to the Duke of Courland. They move slowly and ponderously to suggest their age and the important positions of the Capulets and the duke, the self-importance of the nurse, and the religious dignity of the friar. They "speak" by deliberate gestures, as if they were declaiming. When Lady Capulet finds Tybalt dead, she indulges in all the most time-honored ways of mourning—beating her breast, raising her hands to heaven, and so on.

To some extent this style of movement is dictated by the music. Prokofiev has written heavily accented melodramatic scenes for these parts, in contrast with the passionately lyrical passages for the lovers or the gentler melodies for the friar, whose unsurprising mime gestures—hands folded or

arms raised in prayer and other ritualistically inspired movements—flow smoothly as a result. Mime always follows the
rhythm and mood of music.

Because of this, and the type of music she is given, the
part of Juliet is far more dependent on silent acting than on
mimetic gesture. She, far more than Romeo, has to bear the
burden of the drama by the way she develops the role. She
has to move from childish thoughtlessness to passionate
abandon, from bewilderment and despair to tragic decision
and her final suicide. Most of this is conveyed through her
general movements and facial expression, but now and then
deliberate gesture does come into play. When her mother
asks her to join the rest of the guests at the ball, she puts a
hand up to her brow and closes her eyes briefly, meaning
that she is feeling faint and headachy. She asks her nurse
who Romeo is, in the familiar way, by pointing to him and
spreading her hands in inquiry, and she pleads with her
father with clasped hands raised, as unhappy heroines have
done through the ages. She tells Friar Laurence she will kill
herself, again using a traditional gesture—plunging an imaginary dagger into her heart.

The greatest test for this danced Juliet is in the potion
scene, just as it is for the Juliet who has to tackle Shakespeare's marvelous soliloquy. This scene in the ballet is a
mimed soliloquy, and all the powers of communication of
the dancer are brought into play. By bodily and facial control and expression she has to tell us that she is going to take
the sleeping potion and that she is afraid. Unlike Juliet in
the play, she has no specific way of describing her fears or
her doubts about the friar's sincerity: that he may have given
her a poison or that even if he has not, she may wake too
soon and be "stifled in the vault" or so terrified by the sight
of the newly buried Tybalt and the skeletons of her ances-

Margot Fonteyn in *Romeo and Juliet* (Royal Ballet)

tors that she will lose her reason. None of this can be expressed exactly by the dancer of Juliet, but she must convey the *mood* and the *spirit* of these doubts and fears by her acting. Then she drinks the potion resolutely. Immediately she feels sick and ill, drags herself to her bed and onto it before she is overcome by the drug. The scene can be played merely passably, so that it seems to be punctuated by pauses when nothing much is happening, or it can be invested with such passionate understanding that it becomes a highlight of the ballet.

In comedy, there are very different problems to be resolved. A good many balletic comedies include a pair of high-spirited young lovers, and here the characters are similar, but the mood and style, again, vary. Swanilda and Franz in *Coppélia*, Lise and Colas in Ashton's *La Fille mal Gardée,* the mistress of ceremonies and the junior cadet in Lichine's *Graduation Ball*—all are charming young couples who in each case are up against the older generation. But the dancers have to be careful to distinguish them from each other.

The pair with greatest depth are Lise and Colas. In the second act they have one scene which gives them a chance to show more character than the others can. Lise, thinking herself alone, mimes her dream of a wedding and a family of three; Colas, overhearing, has to comfort her embarrassment when she realizes he is there.

Lise's mime in this scene has a special claim for mention. The choreography for this version of *La Fille mal Gardée* is new, by Frederick Ashton, but for the mime scene he enlisted the cooperation of the great ballerina Tamara Karsavina. She had learned and danced the ballet before her Diaghilev Ballet days, when she was at the Maryinsky Theater in St. Petersburg (now the Kirov in Leningrad), in the version which had been choreographed by Jean Dauberval in Bordeaux in 1786—just before the French Revolution—and later produced with revised choreography and equally immense success in Russia. So the mime scene that Karsavina reconstructed for the Royal Ballet Lise is perhaps the oldest we can now see.

It is startlingly clear. Lise gestures with both hands to show a long gown, bending and stretching her hands out to show a train lying on the ground; she raises her hands above her head and lowers an imaginary veil over her face. She puts on an imaginary ring on her wedding finger, hooks her arm into that of an invisible bridegroom, and takes a few steps with him. Then, coming to the other side of the stage, she looks slightly alarmed, moves her hands forward and curving downward to indicate pregnancy, and raises one finger, then a second, then a third. Then she measures three different heights from the ground and looks at her imaginary children. She touches the eldest one and opens an imaginary book and pretends to be teaching—right forefinger raised. One child is naughty; she looks cross, lays it over her knee, and spanks it. The youngest tumbles over; she runs to pick it up and comfort it and then carries it in her arms over to the sheaves of corn (where Colas is hiding), lays it down, and covers it with her shawl.

Lise and Colas, like the young people in *Graduation Ball*, are contrasted with an elderly couple. In each case the elderly woman was created by a male dancer, and this brings us to an important theme in comic mime: the playing of an older female character by a man.

In England this type of acting *en travesti* is usually thought of as playing the dame—not dame in the American sense, but in English pantomime dame sense—and sometimes it is thought of as a particularly odd and English style;

Nadia Nerina and Stanley Holden in *La Fille mal Gardée*
(Royal Ballet)

but it is not confined to England. The original Widow Simone in *La Fille mal Gardée,* in 1786, was a man; the original Carabosse, the witch in *The Sleeping Beauty,* in St. Petersburg in 1890, was Enrico Cecchetti; when Les Ballets des Champs-Élysées produced *La Sylphide,* a male dancer played the witch Madge; and *Graduation Ball* was first given by the Original Ballet Russe with Borislav Runanine as the headmistress.

Playing the dame has tremendous difficulties. The actor-dancer must conceive the character with minute care for action and timing. He must achieve the neatest of balances between being convincingly realistic and outrageously caricatured. Excellent character dancers can fail in this type of part; only if a dancer is completely at home in such a role can he be its perfect interpreter.

A brilliant characterization of this kind is Stanley Holden's Widow Simone for the Royal Ballet—domineering, lovable, boisterous, but delicately timed. The masterpieces, however, in the genre are probably the contrasted characters of the two stepsisters in Ashton's *Cinderella,* created with inspiration and developed over the years by Ashton himself and Robert Helpmann. These two are now, of course, both knights, director of the Royal Ballet and artistic director of the Australian Ballet respectively, but they are blessedly uninhibited by honors and responsibilities.

Separately and together these portraits are worth minute study by anyone interested in gesture and silent acting. Basically the two roles draw together most of the threads of mime in classical ballet. They use traditional gesture, spontaneous gesture, movement and gesture drawn from the commedia dell'arte, and also from the slapstick pantomime of music hall and silent film. They use hand movements, head movements, facial expression, and character makeup,

Robert Helpmann and Frederick Ashton in *Cinderella*
(Royal Ballet)

and all this expresses characters conceived in depth and additionally portrayed throughout by silent acting which gives reality and, at times, pathos to the narrative.

Each of the stepsisters is a complete whole, but they are also so created and handled that they work as a partnership. They complement each other; they "play to" each other, feeding each other with gags and timing their actions so accurately that each performance is highlighted by the other.

The ballet opens with their sitting at each side of a table working at embroidery. Immediately, from makeup and clothes and manner, they are recognizable as a dominating character (Helpmann) and a more retiring and timid one (Ashton). As the action progresses, this impression is implemented—but we discover all kinds of additional qualities, all completely within character, in both. The domineering sister enjoys life, has a tremendous childlike zest for all that comes her way, grabs at the biggest and showiest of everything, whether it is a fan, an orange, or an escort. She has an occasional kindly, tolerant impulse toward her rather tryingly backward sister and the resilient quality that suggests she will never be set back for long by any reverse of fortune. The retiring sister (Ashton) is on the face of it an object for sympathy because of her timid attitude to life and the fact that her sister bosses her, but she has a strong streak of obstinacy and a petulant temper that destroy any illusion of "niceness."

Now these two characters are so mastered by their creators that they are able to play them with complete naturalness and ease—so much so that they hardly seem the brilliant achievements that they in fact are. They hold the balance between convincing humanity and comic caricature per-

151

fectly. They time each movement and gesture with almost breathtaking accuracy.

Take their great scene of preparing for the ball. Preparing for a ball or something equivalent, by the way, is one of the universally favorite subjects for mime. Audiences everywhere seem to delight in watching dancers pretending to dress up and make up in exaggerated mimicry of the way they themselves dress up and make up for a big social occasion. The stepsisters preparing for the ball are an essential and popular scene in all versions of *Cinderella,* and when the sisters are played by men, there is the added fun of recognizing well-observed moments of feminine routines.

In the Ashton-Helpmann performance, it is astonishing to realize how much is packed into a short space of music, which is all that is available. They choose hats; they put on their shoes, have initial difficulty in walking in them; they put on their wigs—so characteristic—black with curled sides and top for Helpmann, sandy-red rising to a high peak for Ashton; they scramble for jewelry (Helpmann, of course, getting all of it); they practice a gavotte with a dancing master, each one trying to monopolize his attention—and this is superb dance mime because every moment is worked out on two levels, the present-action level and the deeper development-of-character level; we have learned a good deal more about the sisters by the end of it. Then boxes of makeup are brought on; they powder, add rouge and lipstick, spray themselves with scent, and are off, arm in arm, to a dress fitting.

Sound mime, either in tragedy or comedy, like great dancing, stands the test of repeated viewing, even if it varies very little from one occasion to another. But the most compulsive enchantment is distilled by the inventive mime who continually revises and amplifies the detail within his created character; under this kind of spell one is drawn again and again into the theater, eager to see for oneself each impromptu brainwave. Spontaneous alteration and addition, however, are only successful in the hands of the master mime; only the most firmly stated theme can support endless complex variations.

Completely different problems face the dancer who portrays another stock comedy character—the simpleton. The prime example in the current repertoire is probably Alain in *La Fille mal Gardée*—the retarded son of the rich farmer Thomas, who is favored by Lise's mother as a prospective son-in-law. The choreographer has helped a great deal in matching Alain's movements to the sometimes hesitant, sometimes exuberant, music of his role, but there are many other elements in Alexander Grant's masterly creation. There is the stance—at every point turned inward. There is the makeup—face and hair uniformly pale so as to emphasize the eyes, and it is through the eyes that Alain's character— slow, sly, gleeful, or sorrowful—shows its various moods. The key to the simpleton, as to the dame, is timing; by timing, the dancer of Alain must show his hesitancy or his bravado, his setbacks or his fits of confidence. But again like the dame, it needs a quality of spirit which enjoys the part it has to play. No one can play dame or simpleton against the grain. Interestingly, there is one notable tradition outside classical ballet altogether with which Alain and his fellows are linked: in Spanish dance. A comedy *jota* frequently treats of a village simpleton often at the mercy of gay young women (as Alain is in the harvesting scene) and who is almost always a very endearing and disarming character.

Where minor parts are concerned, there are a good many types in classical ballet on which variations exist. There are

Alexander Grant, Stanley Holden, and Leslie Edwards in
La Fille mal Gardée (Royal Ballet)

the parents, from the royal couple in *The Sleeping Beauty* or the princess mother in *Swan Lake*, via Clara's parents in *The Nutcracker* to Juliet's father and mother. They have much in common. They all are subsidiary roles, all with some specific purpose, but with very little chance to create individual characters. They have to be capable of taking the stage purposefully for short essential scenes but also capable of reducing themselves to decorative figures during the rest of the action. There are the children—not many of them but mostly rather pretentious, rather spoiled, and rather coy. There are the fussy old men—the tutor and the steward and the lawyer, usually a butt of the young; and there is the local authority, whether duke or burgomaster, who organizes or patronizes at need. There is the priestly or scholarly type, stooping and spectacled, and the army officer, from lieutenant to general.

The dancer's task with all these roles is to hit on the right way of presenting them. The kings and queens must be convincingly regal, and they must move and behave as they would have done in whichever period or environment they are supposed to be living—and so on, through the entire range of characters. In this characterization, gesture, of course, plays its part, because gestures vary according to country and century and costume, as well as according to age group and temperament, but many of these gestures belong to deportment and manners—ways of moving, of using costume accessories, of greeting people—rather than to conveying meaning without speech.

On the whole, dancers do not say very much about how they conceive and interpret roles in dramatic or traditional ballets, but now and then some interviewer stimulates them to something worth remembering. Albert Kahn, in *Days with Ulanova,* quotes her about Giselle:

> My Giselle was conceived as follows: a young, carefree girl in love and convinced of her happiness experiences a great tragedy and in the end develops into the tragic image of a woman with a great, suffering heart. . . . I sought instinctively for that something, that "magic word" if you like, that would turn me into Giselle and make me live her tragedy and believe in it so utterly as to make the audience believe in it too.

Fonteyn, in *The Art of Margot Fonteyn* by Keith Money, says: "In any ballet, a certain amount comes out in rehearsals for me, then when I start performances it is advanced one stage further. As I go on doing performances, in some strange way these things form themselves." She, too, emphasizes the reality her characters have for her: "I know Giselle very well; her friends; where she lives; the trees with the sun shining through the branches. . . . For me, Juliet and her family are so very real that there is still an enormous amount to be explored in that role."

This is how two of the greatest exponents of silent acting regard the work of creation. There is the understanding of the character, the continual development through performance, and, above all, the belief, the feeling of reality, at the center. The performances we see are the fruit of a dance and mime technique which has been completely mastered and given life by the artist. "Look for the life in the character" is what Dame Edith Evans was told when she was an apprentice actress. It is what all the really great theatrical performers do, and it is what we in the audience must do if we are going to estimate properly the value of a portrayal.

Dame Edith Evans has, in fact, given very recently a tremendous demonstration of silent acting. Although *The Whis-*

perers was not a silent film and her role had plenty of dialogue, her mime, in those scenes where the lonely poor old woman is by herself at home, showed with remarkable clarity the power of controlled facial expression, of perfectly conceived character movement. On this high level, the skills of the actor, the dramatic dancer, the pantomimist, the silent film artist, and the circus clown fuse together into one great art of theatrical communication: mime.

Part IV

MIME IN DAILY LIFE

How much do we find mime, or significant gestures, used in everyday life?

A wealth of gesturing goes on, of course, to accompany speech, particularly in the Latin countries. Most of us do it more, or less, according to our temperaments. There is a whole psychology built up on individual gestures, the kinds people use, and why they use them, analyzed and studied and applied to the task of estimating character and helping solve emotional problems by the psychologists and psychiatrists. Books exist about it, and whether or not you find their arguments convincing depends on your individual opinion.

The reasons why people use gestures at all when they talk and the reasons why they use the particular gestures they do are matters for discussion; the gestures themselves are not in question. Some are gestures of emphasis. They can be head or hand gestures, and they act as an underlining of what has been said. They can be quick or ponderous according to the style of speech. They vary enormously, from the public speaker who pounds with his fist on a table as he elaborates his points, as if he hoped to pound them into the heads of his listeners, to the quick exasperated one-hand flick that goes with an ejaculation like "Oh, I forgot all about it!" Some are purely nervous gestures, nail biting, ear pull-

ing, and the like, and have no relation to speech at all. Some
relate to words rather in the way that words can relate to
sounds. Just as some onomatopoeic word, like buzzing, describes the sound it means, so certain gestures describe the
word that is said. People will often draw in the air some
shape to echo what they are saying: a large square box,
and their hands will outline something large and square to
go with the phrase; a spiral staircase, and one hand will
spiral upward to match; go around, and instinctively one
hand will make a circular movement. Instincts like these
come from some basic distrust of verbal communication
handed down from past millennia—some ancient feeling that
the person you are talking to won't grasp what you mean
unless he has some visual translation of the words. But these
gestures don't, of course, take the place of speech normally.

I say normally because they are exactly the kinds of gestures that one does have recourse to in a foreign country
where one doesn't speak the language. You arrive, a foreigner
without a word of the local language, in some remote part
of a country—Japan, for instance—where no one speaks any
language you've ever learned. You have to communicate,
somehow. I don't think you would even hesitate before you
plunged into gestures. First, the pointing ones—me, you, that
house, that fruit, that way. Then, soon after, the relatively
straightforward actions—to drink, to lie down, to sleep, to be
cold (you shiver and fold your arms around yourself), to be
hot (you mop your brow, fan your face, pant slightly). Then
you would make little sentences: you, me, give, that fruit,
to eat, adding a query; a query has always to be made by
facial expression, raised eyebrows, and so on.

This is the way all the explorers had to behave when they
made landfalls on distant continents and islands and met the
local native tribes. They had to be very quick and inventive,

sometimes to save their lives. How do you convey to strange people that you are a friend, come in peace, that you are not going to be dangerous to them so that they should kill you before you can kill them? The explorers had to find an answer to that and so took the risk of casting down weapons, holding out arms, pointing you, me, and shaking one hand with the other to signify friendship.

One of the most interesting developments in the use of mimetic gesture to get over language difficulties is American Indian sign language. This remarkable system meant that the various tribes had a common method of communication, even though their tribal dialects were incomprehensible to one another. They could discuss mutual problems, indulge in trade, exchange news about hunting grounds by means of an elaborate vocabulary of hand movements, worked out in great detail.

No one seems to know much about the origins of this gesture language, and this is a pity, but at least a great many of the gestures themselves have been recorded, partly perhaps because white settlers learned and used a good deal of it in the opening up of the country. Some of the gestures have a variety of different meanings—presumably they become clear in context; otherwise they could lead to great confusion. A good many have a strictly limited meaning— they would have to be learned specifically; they could never be guessed at, as, for instance, the movement meaning "white man," when the right forefinger is drawn across the forehead from left to right, indicating the white man's hat. Many of the action gestures, however, are easily understandable and very similar to gestures in various mime languages: sleep (the head resting with eyes closed, sideways, on the fingers of the left hand which are laid in the palm of the right hand); drink (a hand cupped and raised to the mouth); cry (the forefingers tracing the path of tears down the cheeks from the corners of the eyes).

Some words are made up of two or three gestures. For "ice" the procedure is to sign "water" (that is the same sign as "drink"), then "cold" (fists are held in front of the chest and shaken as if shivering), then "river" (right forefinger drawn to the right across the face until it is level with the right shoulder, and then "freeze over" (for which you hold both hands even with your shoulders, fingers pointing forward, backs up, and move them together slowly). Obviously, it would take a lot of concentration either to use this combination of signs or to grasp it if someone else did it!

What are the other conditions that make us fall back on gesture as a means of communication rather than on words? Distance does it—if we are playing some outdoor sport and are rather far away from each other, too far for our voices to carry, or with the wind blowing in the wrong direction. Any circumstances under which our normal hearing is affected do it—underwater, for instance, or where some deafening noise is going on, on a factory floor, or at a fairground. Circumstances where speech would be disturbing to other people's concentration do it—we've all seen people come in late to a lecture, and quite a pantomime perhaps goes on. Someone tries to indicate seats to them; they indicate in return that they will stand at the back and not bother anyone. A conductor of music uses gesture, with baton and hand, because he could hardly accompany the music the orchestra is playing with a running commentary of vocal instructions. Religious rituals use symbolic gestures to heighten the solemnity of the occasion. Emotional gestures are made by most of us when, as the old phrase has it, "words fail us."

Some spheres of life have rudiments of gesture language peculiar to them. Traffic direction is one of these. It varies in different countries, but its purposes are always the same: the hands and arms of the traffic policeman are used, in gestures that appear in the appropriate handbooks, to direct traffic straight ahead, to the left and right, to stop it, or start it. The drivers of vehicles have recognized signals to use if their automatic signals fail, to indicate left or right turns, to show that they want either to stop or to overtake and pass or are willing to be passed by some vehicle behind. Pedestrians even have one or two gestures: They can hail a bus or they can signal to cars to stop. In Rome, for instance, if you have the courage to try it, you can walk out into the traffic with your hand raised, palm outward, at right angles to the wrist, in that familiar repelling gesture—and cars will stop for you! And pedestrians can, of course, thumb for a hitch.

One very complete system of gesture communication is the ticktack code used by bookmakers at racecourses in England. This is a system of timesaving signals which take the place of the old fashioned runners who carried information about bets and odds for backing horses. The idea originated in Australia toward the end of the last century, and although there is more than one version, the most widely popular is called Piney's.

The general idea is that the bookmakers, who take up their positions at strategic points where they can see one another, signal information with great speed. There are signs for numbers, because each horse is recognizable by its number on the race card; for number one they touch the top of

the head with the tips of the fingers of the right hand, and
so on. Then there are signs for the prices: 33–1 is shown by
crossing the arms and hands across the chest (very like the
gesture the ballerina uses for mother!). The V sign, which
Winston Churchill made world famous during World War
II as the sign of confidence in victory, is the ticktack gesture
for message received clearly.

Gestures are used at auction sales, but apparently there
is nothing worked out about these; people do what they like.
It is largely a question of catching the auctioneer's eye and
then making *some* kind of gesture—pulling your earlobe or
putting your finger against your nose. In consequence, there
is a belief among most people who rarely go to auctions
that you are almost bound to be sold something you don't
want simply because out of nervousness you have scratched
your head or licked your lips!

Underwater swimming employs some gestures that are
fairly universally understood, even though there is no recognized international code. These range from the familiar
pointing for "me" or "you" or "that" to the distress gesture,
in which the closed fist is waved in a semicircle from shoulder to shoulder, passing in front of the face each time. One
remembers some of the gestures seen in movies with underwater sequences like *Thunderball:* the thumb-up sign for
"I am going up" or the hand raised with forefinger and
thumb making a circle and the rest of the fingers pointing
upward for "all's well."

In judo there is a recognized signal for defeat; in prize-
fights the victor clasps his hands above his head; in karate
there are salutations rich in traditional political significance,
as well as in respect for teachers and opponents.

A very different sphere of gesture lies in conducting music.
This is divided between the baton, which is held in the right

hand, and the left hand. The baton gives the beat—there are set patterns for indicating one, two, three, or four beats in a bar. The basic pattern is kept, with subdivisions, for compound time. The baton also starts and stops the music—to stop, the conductor brings it straight down sharply or slowly, whichever is needed, pausing for a second at the end of the gesture before he lowers his arm to his side. The quality of his gestures, too—strong or gentle—signifies the dynamics—that is, the loudness or softness of sound—and it shows articulation—that is, whether the music flows smoothly on or whether it is accented. His left hand and arm have another function. The kinds of gestures they employ are the universal gesture of appeal—arm out, palm up, for a full strong sound; palm down for a quiet passage; or the slow upward and outward movement for crescendo; the slow downward and inward movement for diminuendo.

Religious gesture belongs to every creed and denomination, although some have more specific gestures than others. Christians, of course, make the sign of the cross, either toward themselves or toward others: from the forehead downward, then across from shoulder to shoulder. A priest raises the first two fingers of his right hand in blessing or lays his hands on someone's head. He clasps or lays his hands together palm to palm when he prays. A Buddhist puts his hands palm to palm, then raises them to forehead level, and touches his brow with the joined thumbs as he prays. A Hindu lifts the hands even higher, above his head. A Moslem has twelve positions united to different moments in his daily prayers. He stands to face Mecca; he raises his hands to his head, palms forward, thumbs touching his earlobes; he puts his joined hands, right over left, over his breast; he kneels and touches the ground with his forehead—these and other gestures are significantly linked to his devotions. The methods of communication in the silent religious orders have ancient traditions—although, no doubt, as with American Indian sign language, which has evolved signs for record players and television sets, new gestures creep in. The basic ones remain the same—gestures such as the Trappist circle, made by touching tips of thumbs and tips of forefingers, meaning God. Has this, one wonders, a distant relationship to the one-handed circle of the Romans which meant love?

One immensely important sphere where gestures are used in everyday life is in dealing with the deaf and dumb. The various institutions in Europe and America have different views on the best manual language. There are two—single hand (favored in the United States) and double hand (favored in Europe). Both are based on the alphabet; a different set position of the hand or hands signifies each letter of the alphabet, and words are spelled out in this way. Television programs for the deaf use these methods together with a slowly spoken text which can be lip-read by the viewer, and religious services for the deaf are also couched in gesture language.

The need for theatrical performances for deaf audiences has long been recognized and to some extent met, but in recent years really fascinating developments have been taking place. In England the Royal National Institute for the Deaf established a mime group half a dozen years ago, whose success is largely due to Pat Keysell, their teacher and producer. This attractive young woman, who also conducts a weekly BBC television program for deaf children, has a knowledge of different mime styles that has made it possible for the group to stage scenes with contemporary significance—they have even tackled the space race—and make a real impact on local audiences who have never come in contact with mime before.

This group is, however, amateur; an even more interesting venture has been launched in the United States—a National Theater of the Deaf. For this, various interested people ranging from stage directors to Japanese dancers to experts in tumbling and fencing have come together to create a professional organization. Its origins are noteworthy because, like so many other vital ideas, it emerged from a combination of individual enthusiasms which came together just at a good time to promote their dream.

The strands were made up of an actress—Anne Bancroft, who had studied manual language for her compelling performance in *The Miracle Worker,* the film about Helen Keller; a psychologist concerned for the deaf, Dr. Edna Levine; and the commissioner of the U.S. Vocational Rehabilitation Administration, Mary Switzer. Together they recruited experienced theater people willing to take the idea further; with the support of the federal government, the company found a place at the Eugene O'Neill Memorial Theater Foundation in Connecticut.

Opening with an NBC television program, at which soliloquies and poems were given in manual language, with a narrator to explain to the uninitiated what the deaf could understand by signs, the company has now built up a repertoire. It comprises mime plays (ranging from Saroyan to kabuki), adaptations of comic operas, and poetry reading, all tackled by this company of deaf actors with freedom and ease.

Significant gesture has always had its part in everyday social life, more so, of course, in earlier centuries. There have always been gestures of contempt and insult, ranging

National Theater of the Deaf in *Gianni Schicchi*

from nose thumbing, "cocking a snook," and thumb biting ("Do you bite your thumb at us, sir?" asks the Montagues' servant Abraham, in *Romeo and Juliet*, when he begins quarreling with the Capulet servants) to the ritual challenges of throwing down the glove before duels. There have equally always been gestures of reverence and service. These have origins in the temples of antiquity—prostration, kneeling, bowing. They extended into polite society and court life, becoming more and more complicated, so that the language of bowing and curtsying gained a considerable vocabulary. In his Delsarte book, Ted Shawn examines the complex implications of different kinds of bowing, and a book about English manners and customs, *The Polite World*, by Joan Wildeblood and Peter Brinson, describes, century by century, the varying and developing art of "the reverence."

Gesture accompanying speech has always been more characteristic of Latin people than any other. Sometimes Anglo-Saxons have sneered at this, implying that the French or Italians gesticulate madly, their arms whirling about with no rhyme or reason; so it is interesting to come across a defense of gesture as used by Italian actors, in Addison McLeod's *Plays and Players in Modern Italy*. He says that this gesture is "not a wild medley but orderly and scientific. It expresses the Italian love for detail and accuracy."

One social gesture language that has been forgotten but was in use in the eighteenth century is the language of the fan. The fan was first adopted in Europe in the seventeenth century; it came greatly into vogue in society, and a system of etiquette was worked out about the ways in which it could be held when not being put to its practical purpose of making a hot atmosphere more endurable. More than that, however, it became an accessory to flirtation, and a woman could convey various sorts of amorous messages by the way she used her fan. A closed fan, held with the tip to the lips meant "Be careful, we can be overheard"; held horizontally, the tip pointing to the heart, it meant "I love you"; held with the tip touching the forehead, it meant "You must be out of your mind." If the tip touched the right cheek, it meant yes, if the left cheek, no. The open fan had a similar repertoire of phrases. If you hid your eyes with it, you said, "I love you"; if you held it pointed down and made quick brushing-away movements with it, you said, "I do *not* love you." And the reason for this language? Obviously it was a little like the secret writing or ciphers children sometimes indulge in for amusement. This fan language of love must have been preeminently for amusement—to see who was observant enough to pick up your meaning, rather than to make any serious statements. In a society familiar with the language, its communications could hardly be secret.

Social amusements like that are out of date, but taken all in all, we use gestures a good deal. We wave good-bye; we shake or nod our heads for no or yes. We point "you" or "me" or "that." In gesture we say, "You go first," and "Won't you sit down?", "Stop!" and "Come." We lift our eyebrows in inquiry; we shrug if something doesn't matter or can't be helped.

If you look around, you'll be surprised how many gestures are quite instinctive with people. No one thinks of them as mime. But of course, that's what they are; they are to theatrical mime exactly what our everyday speech is to the spoken dialogue of a play.

Part V

PATHS AHEAD

What are the present-day trends in theatrical mime, and what kind of future can it have? Broadly speaking, it can be divided into mime in ballet, mime in plays and operas, dance drama theaters, and pantomime companies.

In ballet, whether it is based on classical dancing or some other dance form, choreographers nowadays almost universally use expressive mime—silent acting—rather than traditional gesture. The exception comes when a ballet with a history is rechoreographed, like *La Fille mal Gardée,* or *Raymonda* or *The Nutcracker,* when the form and score demand some acceptable type of gesture mime in the narrative. Otherwise, silent acting, making a free use of the vocabulary of gesture which is part of the heritage of ballet, is accepted for dramatic ballets. This is a good trend, not really new (at various times in the nineteenth century, choreographers were experimenting in this direction, and Fokine's great ballets brought it very much into play). At present the dramatic ballet is a rather suspect branch of choreography, but there is no reason to suppose that the pendulum will not swing, as pendulums tend to, and revive enthusiasm and admiration for narrative.

We are rarely asked to make dramatic allowances in the way one used to for the shortcomings of singers who have no notion of acting. Thus, in opera, as production has gained naturalism and logic, the standard of mime has become much more generally good. In plays, quite apart from the excellent mime which all good actors make use of in a spoken part, mime continues to be used in production. The mood of the day prefers an imaginative combination of speech, lighting, and mime to the spectacular decors and stage effects of the past.

Dance drama theaters flourish in India and the Far East, and here one finds a curious situation. There are no present-day trends—all is ancient tradition, formalized and immutable—and yet the vivid life and robust character of these theaters make them far more impressively alive and stimulating than the up-to-date or avant-garde Western theater movements.

As for Western pantomime companies, they all are beginning to feel, quite obviously, that changes must come. In *The Theater of Jean-Louis Barrault,* this great mime spoke out forcefully about his art. He said, "I have the feeling that the art of mime is now once more at an impasse," and suggested that Western mime needed a change of direction, that it must find a new mode of expression with more of the scope and force of the Oriental schools.

Certainly this is something to hope for. At present, in the sphere of pure pantomime unlinked to ballet, spoken plays, or opera, there are comedy mimes—the amusing or satirical episodes in a Marceau type of program or the old-fashioned comedy of the Danish Pantomimeteater or the heavily caricatured comedy deriving from the Central European school of the 1930's—and there are pathetic mimes about unobtainable dreams, disappointments, and disillusionments. Watching Marceau is like attending a poetry recital where the realistic and idealistic alternate but where everything is couched in short lyric form; in contrast, the kathakali or Chinese dance drama is a full-length play reminiscent of Elizabethan or Jacobean tragedy.

Efforts are being made in the West to find new roads for pantomime to travel. Barrault suggests, and one can hardly help agreeing, that it needs to become less stereotyped, that too many carbon copies of famous mimes exist. After all, dancers and actors all make very personal use of their basic technical skills, whereas mimes tend to resemble one another rather too closely. There is no need to continue the Deburau-Marceau tradition of the white-faced pantomime artist with his brilliant thumbnail sketches of everyday situations. Each new mime should create his own character and style out of his own individual appearance, physical qualities, and emotional tastes and experiences. The great artists have always created their own characters: Deburau's Pierrot, Rich's Harlequin Lun, Grimaldi's Joey, Chaplin's Charlie, Barrault's Baptiste, Marceau's Bip, Tati's M. Hulot. To echo these characterizations at any point is to weaken the art of pantomime as a whole; to invent some fresh and compelling character of one's own is to strengthen the art.

Barrault's road to the future—although he seems unlikely to take it himself, since it is a good many years since he produced any pantomimes—seems to lie in an amalgam of various substances: the traditional elements which he uses in that famous scene in *Les Enfants du Paradis* and the more modern moods which he and his master Étienne Decroux worked on in the 1930's and 1940's, which Decroux termed "statue mime." This description surely includes Marceau's very fine item *Youth, Maturity, Old Age and Death.* In this he remains on one spot, and by facial expression and stance alone he shows the upward and downward movements of man's progress through life. It is hard to see this type of mime as a fruitful line to follow, but in limited doses it is impressive. Marceau's new school of mime is bound to breathe fresh life into his beloved art, and perhaps from it will emerge new possibilities, as well as new artists. Meanwhile, another Frenchman, Jacques Lecoq, is helping students get a clear view of mime, ridding it of accumulations of mannerisms or unhelpful convention and making them feel that they are discovering a new and flexible art of communication.

Where else can one look for new ideas? Adam Darius, although he continues to use the white makeup of French pantomime, is cleaving an individual path. He has worked in other theatrical media and in many countries and so has a wide experience to draw on. His themes are frequently blazingly up-to-date—a recent one, *Psychedelic*, deals with hippies and LSD. A Soviet mime—like Popov a circus clown —Leonid Jengibarov, has emerged from the ring and has become a theatrical force with a blend of French pantomime and Chaplin-Keaton silent film technique in an individual mold. In Poland, the Wroclaw Pantomime Theater, founded in 1956 by Tommazewski, is a company built without drawing on earlier tradition. They are proud to say that they have not been influenced by much knowledge of their predecessors. Influences, of course, are insidious. Sometimes people are hardly conscious of them, but they creep in. Everyone must train if he is going to be an artist of any kind, and the student-teacher relationship carries its influences from one generation to another.

However, the Wroclaw company has its own ideas of mime, and this makes it interesting. It gives mime dramas of a fairly straightforward character, but it also gives pantomimes without stories. One of these, *The Labyrinth*, is said to "act on our senses by its shape, its pictures, its

Adam Darius

rhythm." In this way it must stand in the same relationship to ordinary mime drama as pure dance ballets do to narrative ballets. Whether this will prove a fruitful path for mime to follow is hard to say; it obviously ties in with Charles Weidman's experimental kinetic pantomimes, and all experiment is bound to be of value in extending the scope of mime and freeing it from convention.

Another company busily developing an individual style is the Mime Group, established in 1953 and now based at the Theater on the Balustrade in Prague, Czechoslovakia. Certainly Ladislav Fialka's *The Fools* is one of the most delightful entertainments ever created in the European mime tradition growing from the commedia dell'arte. Its alternative title is *A Strange Dream of a Clown*—how hard it is to sever connections with those all-pervasive characters, Clown and Pierrot! Perhaps this, more than anything else, makes Western mime seem limited. Fialka's *Fools*, however, is a beautifully knit production in which unrelated scenes are brought together into a unity. It touches briefly on the Bible (Cain and Abel) and on Greek myth (Orpheus), and it has a charming comedy sequence where Hamlet rehearses the players. This suggests that Hamlet asks them for a play, and they offer, in dumb show, one or two other Shakespearean tragic episodes, like Desdemona and Othello, each of which he vetoes before they strike the one he wants—the one portraying the murder of his father.

Another Fialka mime, *The Clowns*, makes one realize how much really clear thinking is needed in mime presentation. It is a historical sketch of pantomime, beginning, charmingly, with the commedia dell'arte (and here many of the traditional bits of business, known as *lazzi*, are used, such as Harlequin catching and eating flies), continuing with a scene from the Deburau era and then a German circus. In the last

Ladislav Fialka group, Prague, in *The Fools*

scene it comes up to date, and as frequently happens in topical and modern-dress mime, it loses its way. The lack of a well-worked-out scenario immediately shows—one idea, the injustices dealt out to the "little man" in peace and war, is drawn out until it becomes a bore.

All these experiments may prove to be contributory factors which can be brought together in some really significant new form. One feels that it must be more of a breakaway than anything we can see at present, more revolutionary in character, more directly a poetic conception of our contemporary life. Poetic it must be—whether lyric or epic, mime, like dancing, is poetic in character and should open the gates of the imagination—but it must be based on modern everyday life as well to have real contact with audiences. It must come in line with the other arts and belong to today, not yesterday or the day before that, as it tends to do. At its most flourishing, Western mime was always topical in reference, and now it needs to be topical in style as well. That is one direction it might well take.

Most mime artists seem unaware that there is one important element in their work which needs strengthening— really substantial scenarios are called for in both solo items and mime plays. All too often they are content to settle for a few good ideas where sustained and solid thinking is really necessary. First-rate scenarios, of course, are as hard to come by as first-rate theatrical plays, and it was largely for lack of scenarios that Barrault stopped staging mime. But there is no real reason why writers should not be found to create plays with mime artists in mind, and this is another development which would inject new life into the art.

Again, Western mime might boldly create a new and freer school of mime drama, and in this it is more than possible that the seed has been sown with that enterprising venture

Ladislav Fialka group, Prague, in *The Road*

in Connecticut, the National Theater of the Deaf. Here, diverse influences have already come together. The company studies acting, modern dance, kabuki; one of them, Bernard Bragg, is a pupil of Marceau. Narrators are used, but the emphasis is on mime and gesture language. Perhaps this is moving toward the kind of development that Barrault envisaged, when mime brings together East and West and climbs out of the rut in which it seems to exist at present.

Obviously, from the reactions of viewers to these programs, something exciting is going on. Critics have talked of "an elaborate and delicate fabric of muscular language that is intensely interesting and achingly moving," of "a brilliant professional troupe of entertainers who have discovered a new and exciting dimension in drama."

Perhaps they have. Perhaps they will be able to point the way for other brilliant and gifted pantomime artists all over the world, mime companies from such divergent geographical areas as Chile and Czechoslovakia, toward movement and development. Then the Western-derived pantomime would take its place as an equal partner with spoken drama, opera, and the ballet and as a challenging, stimulating experience for all of us who love the arts of the theater.

SELECTED BIBLIOGRAPHY

AMBROSE, KAY, *Classical Dances and Costumes of India*. New York, Hillary House, 1957.

BARLANGHY, ISTVAN, *Mime Training and Exercises*. New Rochelle, N.Y., Sportshelf, 1967.

BEARE, WILLIAM, *The Roman Stage*, 3d ed. New York, Barnes & Noble, 1965.

BOWERS, FAUBION, *Theatre in the East*. Camden, N.J., Thomas Nelson, 1956.

BROADBENT, R. J., *A History of Pantomime*. New York, Citadel Press, 1965.

BRUFORD, ROSE, *Teaching Mime*. New York, Barnes & Noble, 1958.

CAULIEZ, A. J., *Cinema d'aujourd'hui: Jacques Tati*. France, Premier Publications, n.d.

CHAMBERS, E. K., *The Elizabethan Stage*. London, Oxford University Press, 1923. 4 vols.

——, *The Medieval Stage*. London, Oxford University Press, 1903. 2 vols.

CHAPLIN, CHARLES, *My Autobiography*. New York, Simon and Schuster, 1964.

CHEN, JACK, *The Chinese Theatre*. Chester Springs, Pa., Dufour, 1950.

DICK, KAY, *Pierrot*. London, Hutchinson, 1960.

GOPAL, RAM, and DADACHANJI, SEROZH, *Indian Dancing*. London, Phoenix House, 1951.

HOFSINDE, ROBERT, *Indian Sign Language*. New York, Morrow, 1956.

HUFF, THEODORE, *Charles Chaplin*. New York, Henry Schuman, 1951.

HUNT, D. and K., *Pantomime*. New York, Atheneum, 1964.

KALVODOVA-SIS-VANIS, *Chinese Theatre*. London, Spring Books, n.d.

LABAN, RUDOLF, *The Mastery of Movement*. London, Macdonald & Evans, 1961.

LAWSON, JOAN, *Mime*. London, Pitman, 1957.

Selected Bibliography

LINDSAY, JACK, *Leisure and Pleasure in Roman Egypt.* New York, Barnes & Noble, 1963.

LUCIAN, "On Pantomime," *Works.* London, Oxford University Press, 1905. 4 vols.

MARASH, JESSIE GRACE, *Mime in Class and Theatre.* London, Harrap, 1950.

MAWER, IRENE, *The Art of Mime.* London, Methuen, 1932.

MEHL, DIETER, A. J., *The Elizabethan Dumb Show.* Cambridge, Harvard University Press, 1965.

NICOLL, ALLARDYCE, *Masks, Mimes and Miracles.* New York, Cooper Square Publishers, 1964.

NOVERRE, J. G., *Letters on Dancing and Ballets,* trans. by C. W. Beaumont. Brooklyn, N.Y., Dance Horizons, n.d.

O'NEILL, P. G., *Early Nō Drama.* London, Lund, Humphries, 1959.

SAYRE, GWENDA, *Creative Miming.* London, Herbert Jenkins, 1959.

SCOTT, A. C., *The Classical Theatre of China.* London, Allen & Unwin, 1957.

———, *The Kabuki Theatre of Japan.* New York, Collier Books, 1965.

SHAWN, TED, *Every Little Movement.* Published by the author, 1954.

SINGHA, RINA, and MASSEY, REGINALD, *Indian Dances.* New York, Braziller, n.d.

SMITH, WINIFRED, *Commedia dell'Arte.* Bronx, N.Y., Benjamin Blom, n.d.

SORELL, WALTER, ed., *The Dance Has Many Faces.* New York, Columbia University Press, 1966.

SELECTED FILMOGRAPHY

Marcel Marceau

Marcel Marceau or L'Art du Mime—France, 1965—black and white. Marceau talks about mime and interprets Bip and Don Juan.

Pantomimes: *Marcel Marceau*—France, 1954—color.
Includes "David and Goliath," "The Butterfly Chase," and "The Lion Tamer."

The Dinner Party—Germany, 1958.

In the Park—France, 1956.

The Overcoat—Germany, 1955—color.

Paris-Montmartre—France, 1950.
With Edith Piaf.

Mic-Mac—France, 1949.

Royaumont—France, 1948.

A program in the Stacheltier series, produced by Defa (East Germany) in 1955, includes "The Overcoat," "Bip and the Bee," "Bip as Tragedian," and style exercises.

Les Enfants du Paradis—France, 1943–45—black and white.
Full-length feature with Jean-Louis Barrault as Deburau; includes a reconstruction of a Pierrot mime from the Théâtre des Funambules.

Full-length features starring Jacques Tati

Jour de Fête—France—black and white.

Les Vacances de Monsieur Hulot—France—black and white.

Mon Oncle—France—color.

The great actors of the silent films are on record. It is impossible to give any comprehensive list. They are frequently to be seen at the specialist cinemas or museums. Two recent compilations

Selected Filmography

of Harold Lloyd's films have been generally distributed: *Harold Lloyd's World of Comedy* (1962) and *Harold Lloyd's Funny Side of Life* (1963). Two recent compilations of Laurel and Hardy have been generally distributed: *The Crazy World of Laurel and Hardy* (1964) and *Laurel and Hardy's Laughing '20's* (1965).

Ladislav Fialka
Few Words Suffice for Love—Czechoslovakia—1961.
Young Footlights—1960—Czechoslovakia—documentary.

Western classical ballet mime occurs in films such as:
The Bolshoi Ballet—Britain, 1957—color.
This includes Galina Ulanova in *Giselle.*
The Bolshoi Ballet in America—U.S.S.R.—black and white.
The Royal Ballet—Britain—1959—color.
This includes Act II of *Swan Lake, The Firebird,* and *Ondine* with Margot Fonteyn.
Romeo and Juliet—Britain, 1965—color.
This stars Margot Fonteyn and Rudolf Nureyev.
Romeo and Juliet—U.S.S.R., 1954—color.
This stars Galina Ulanova.
Othello—U.S.S.R., 1960—color.
The Nutcracker—United States, 1965—color.
Danced by the Stuttgart Ballet.
The Tales of Hoffman—Britain, 1951—color.
In this film Moira Shearer, Ludmilla Tcherina, Robert Helpmann, and Leonide Massine mime their roles, which are sung by opera singers.

India
Bharat Natyam—India—color.
Kathakali—India, 1960—color.
Lord Siva Danced—London, 1948—black and white.
Demonstrations of Bharata-nātya (Bharat Natyam), kathakali, kathak, and manipuri.

China
Chinese Theater—Britain/France, 1960—color.
Four episodes performed by Peking Theater troupe.

Selected Filmography

Training Players for Chinese Classical Theater—China, 1958—
black and white.

The Stage Art of Mei Lan-Fang—China, 1955.
This includes a demonstration by this great Chinese actor.

Japan
Nō Theater.

INDEX

Adam, Adolphe, 140
Africa, 42, 116
Alexandria, 49
Al-Far, Ahmed Fahim, 115
Alhambra Theatre, London, 96
American Ballet Theater, 113
American Indian sign language, 160, 161
Angiolini, Gasparo, 75
Animal pantomime, 133, 134, 135
Apology for My Life (Cibber), 74
Aristophanes, 45
Aristotle, 44
Arlecchino. *See* Harlequin
Art of Margot Fonteyn, The (Money), 156
Art of Mime, The (Mawer), 108
Ashton, Frederick, 27, 92, 135, 140, 146, 149, 151, 152, 153
Augustus, Emperor, 48
Australian aborigines, 42, 44
Australian Ballet, 149
Azuma Kabuki, 60

Balanchine, George, 111, 135, 140
Balasaraswati, 52
Bali, 65, 124, 134
Ballet d'action, 76, 90
Ballon, Jean, 72
Bancroft, Anne, 166
Baptiste, 104
Barrault, Jean-Louis, 77, 104, 171, 172, 177
Bathyllus of Alexandria, 49
Beare, William, 47
Beaumont, Cyril W., 90
Beerbohm, Max, 96
Bentley, Muriel, 113
Berk, Ernest, 108

Bharata Muni, 51, 52
Bharata-nātya, 51, 52, 60
Bip at a Society Party, 106
Birds, The (Aristophanes), 45
Birth of a Nation, 38
Blasis, Carlo, 90
Bolm, Adolph, 50, 101
Boutique Fantasque, La, 102
Bragg, Bernard, 115, 179
Brinson, Peter, 168
Broadbent, R. J., 81
Bucco, 65
Burma, 125, 134

Camargo, Marie-Anne Cupis de, 72
Cambodia, 130
Carré, Michel, 96
Carnaval, 50, 102
Casorti, Pasqual, 85
Catarina, 89
Cecchetti, Enrico, 90, 149
Central European Dance, 93, 95, 108, 110, 171
Cercle Funambulisque, 99
Ceylon, 64, 65
Chaliapin, Feodor, 91
Champs-Élysées, Ballets des, 149
Chaney, Lon, 38
Chaplin, Charles, 38, 40, 41, 106, 110, 172, 173
Chauvel, Charles and Elsa, 44
Cheshire, Harold, 108
China, 28, 52, 53, 85, 87, 124, 128, 130, 131, 132, 133, 138
Chinese Theatre (Kalvodova-sisvanis), 132
Christensen, Lew, 113
Cibber, Colley, 74
Cilicia, 49

Index

Cinderella, 27, 50, 149, 151, 152
City Lights, 38
Clown, 65, 76, 79, 81, 138, 175
Clowns, circus, 83
Clowns, The, 175
Clytemnestra, 113
Columbine, 67, 85, 102
Come Dance with Me (De Valois), 99
Commedia dell'arte, 65, 67, 68, 85, 95, 121, 149, 175. See also Clown, Columbine, Harlequin, Pantaloon, Pierrot, Punchinello
Compagnie des Quinze, 104
Compagnie Madeleine-Renaud-Jean-Louis-Barrault, 104
Cooper, Gary, 33
Copeau, Jean, 104
Coppélia, 29, 30, 31, 32, 33, 34, 35, 126, 128, 146
Coq d'Or, Le, 92
Corneille, 72
Courtès, Papa, 99
Crossroads, The, 87
Czechoslovakia, 175

Dance and Drama in Bali (De Zoete), 134
Dance Has Many Faces, The, 111
Darius, Adam, 115, 173
Dauberval, Jean, 76, 90, 147
Daumier, 77
Days with Ulanova (Kahn), 156
Deaf, National Theater of the, 115, 166, 179
Deaf, Royal National Institute for the, 165
Deaf and dumb language, 165
Deburau, Jean Gaspard, 76, 77, 81, 104, 172, 175
Decroux, Étienne, 104, 172
Delos, 45
Delsarte, François, 92, 93, 95, 106, 110, 113, 168
De Maine, Duchesse, 72
De Mille, Agnes, 113, 140
Denishawn, 113

Denmark, 85, 171
De Valois, Ninette, 91, 99, 110, 140
De Zoete, Beryl, 134
Diaghilev Ballet, 90, 92, 100, 146
Dick, Kay, 77
Dickens, Charles, 81
Didelot, Charles Louis, 76, 90
Display, The, 135
Don Giovanni, 91
Don Quixote, 111
Drury Lane Theatre, London, 75, 81
Dumb shows, Elizabethan, 68, 69, 71, 72
Duncan, Isadora, 93
Dunham, Katherine, 116

Egypt, 48, 49, 50, 111, 115
Elssler, Fanny, 89
Empire Theatre, London, 96
L'Enfant Prodigue, 96, 99, 108, 111
Enfants du Paradis, Les, 104, 115, 172
England, 54, 55, 68, 69, 71, 72, 74, 75, 76, 79, 81, 95, 96, 108, 110, 165
Enters, Angna, 111
Eoline, 89
Epicharmus of Sicily, 46
Esmeralda, 89
Et Puis, Bonsoir, 108
Eugene O'Neill Memorial Theater Foundation, 166
Evans, Edith, 156, 157
Every Little Movement (Shawn), 93, 168
Everyman, 55

Faithless Wife, The, 47
Fall River Legend, 140, 142
Fan language, 169
Fialka, Ladislav, 175
Fille mal Gardée, La (Ashton), 27, 110, 135, 146, 147, 153, 170
Fille mal Gardée, La (Dauberval), 76, 90, 146, 149
Films, 38, 40, 41
Firebird, The, 135

Index

Foire de Saint-Germain, 67

Foire de Saint-Laurent, 67

Fokine, Michel, 100, 101, 102, 135, 170

Folies Nouvelles, Paris, 96

Fonteyn, Margot, 142, 143, 156

Fools, The, 175

Forains, 67

Forest, The, 116

France, 28, 67, 68, 72, 76, 77, 92, 93, 96, 99, 100, 104, 106, 171, 172, 173

Fugitive, The, 110

Funambules, Théâtre de, Paris, 76, 77, 96

Gaîté Parisienne, 102

Garrick, David, 74, 137

Gautier, Théophile, 89

Geltser, Vassily, 91

Genée, Adeline, 96

General, The, 38

Gerdt, Paul, 90

Giselle, 12, 13, 14, 15, 17, 18, 19, 20, 22, 23, 24, 25, 101, 126, 156

Gluck, Christoph Willibald, 76, 91

Gold Rush, The, 38, 40, 41

Gorboduc, 68

Gore, Walter, 110

Graduation Ball, 146, 147

Graham, Martha, 113

Grahn, Lucile, 89

Grant, Alexander, 153

Great Devil, The, 81

Greece, 44, 45, 48, 56, 64, 111, 136

Grimaldi, Joseph, 76, 79, 81, 85, 172

Grisi, Carlotta, 89

Guinea, African Ballet of, 116

Habima Theater, Israel, 115

Hamlet, 58, 68, 69, 71

Harlequin, 67, 72, 74, 76, 77, 85, 102, 104, 121, 175

Harlequin's Mechanical Statue, 85

Harold Lloyd's World of Comedy, 38

Helpmann, Robert, 50, 92, 110, 135, 149, 151, 152

Herodas of Kos, 46

Hilverding, Franz van Wewen, 75, 90

Hinkson, Mary, 116

History of Mimes and Pantomimes (Weaver), 75

History of Pantomime (Broadbent), 81

Holden, Stanley, 149

Hovey, Mrs. Richard, 93

Howard, Andrée, 110

Illustrated London News, 99

Imperial Ballet, St. Petersburg, 90, 100

In the Park, 106

Inbal, Israel, 115

India, 21, 22, 27, 51, 52, 60, 61, 63, 64, 65, 124, 125, 126, 129, 134, 137

Institute of Mime, London, 108

Intolerance, 38

Iran, 115

Israel, 115

Italy, 67, 90, 168. *See also* Rome

Izumo, 58

Japan, 56, 58, 60, 65, 124, 129

Java, 65

Jengibarov, Leonid, 173

Jesters, 54

Jongleurs, 54

Jooss, Kurt, 108

Jour de Fête, 106

Julius Caesar, 48

Justinian, Emperor, 51

Kabuki, 58, 60, 65, 129

Kahn, Albert, 156

Kalvodova-sis-vanis, 132

Karno, Fred, 40

Karsavina, Tamara, 101, 146, 147

Kathak, 60

Index

Kathakali, 60, 61, 63, 64, 65
Kaye, Nora, 113
Kchessinska, Mathilde, 90
Keaton, Buster, 38, 106, 110, 173
Keller, Helen, 166
Kelly, Emmett, 83
Kemp, Lindsay, 108
Kerala Kalamandalam, 61, 63, 64
Keysell, Pat, 165
Khon, 65, 129
Kirov Ballet, Leningrad, 146
Komisarjevsky, 104
Korea, 56
Kos, 46
Kuchipudi, 60

Labyrinth, The, 173
Lady into Fox, 110
Lady of the Camellias, 113
Laing, Hugh, 113
Lakhon, 65, 129
Langdon, Harry, 38
Larcher brothers, 99
Larsen, Niels Bjørn, 85
La Scala, Milan, 90
Lawson, Joan, 121
Lecoq, Jacques, 173
Leisure and Pleasure in Roman Egypt (Lindsay), 50
Letters on Dancing and Ballets (Noverre), 75, 136, 137
Levine, Dr. Edna, 166
Lichine, David, 146
Lilac Garden, 110, 113
Limon, José, 113
Lincoln's Inn Fields, London, 74
Lindsay, Jack, 50
Little Hump-backed Horse, The, 91
Littlefield, Catherine, 113
Livius Andronicus, 48
Lloyd, Harold, 38
Loring, Eugene, 113
Louis XIV of France, 72
Louther, William, 116
Lucian of Samosata, 49, 50, 120
Lun. *See* Rich, John

Maccus, 65
MacKaye, Steele, 93, 110
MacMillan, Kenneth, 27, 89, 140
Mahabharata, 61, 125
Maker of Masks, The, 106
Makeup, 136, 137, 138
Malabar, 60
Malinche, La, 113
Manipuri, 66
Marceau, Marcel, 28, 68, 77, 104, 106, 122, 133, 171, 172, 173, 179
Marigny, Théâtre de, Paris, 104
Marriage of Figaro, The, 91
Mars and Venus, 74, 75
Maryinsky Theater, St. Petersburg, 90, 146
Masks, 135, 136
Massine, Leonide, 92, 102
Mastery of Movement, The (Von Laban), 37
Mawer, Irene, 108
May, Jane, 96, 99
McLeod, Addison, 168
Meng, 52, 54
Midsummer Night's Dream, A, 111
Minstrels, 54
Miracle in the Gorbals, 110
Miracle plays, 55
Miracle Worker, The, 166
Molin, Francisque, 74
Money, Keith, 156
Monkey, 134
Mon Oncle, 106
M. Hulot's Holiday, 106
Moor's Pavane, The, 113
Morality plays, 55
Moreton, Ursula, 99
Motokiyo, Se-ami, 56, 58
Music conducting, 164
Mystery plays, 55

Nero, Emperor, 48
New York City Ballet, 111
Night Shadow, 111
Nijinsky, Vaslav, 50, 101
Nō theater, 56, 58, 60, 65, 129

Index

Noverre, Jean Georges, 75, 76, 90, 136, 137
Nureyev, Rudolf, 142
Nutcracker, The, 111, 155, 170

Offenbach, Jacques, 92
O Kuni of Izumo, 58
Ondine, 110, 140
On Mime (Enters), 110
On Pantomime (Lucian), 49, 50
Opera, 91
Operetta, 127, 128
Original Ballet Russe, 149
Orpheus and Eurydice, 91
Otero, La Belle, 100
Overcoat, The, 104

Pagan Greece, 111
Page, Ruth, 113
Pakistan, 60
Pantaloon, 65
Pantomimeteater, Copenhagen, 85, 171
Pantomimes, English, 95
Pappus, 65
Pavlova, Anna, 101, 113
Peking Opera, 85, 87
Perrot, Jules, 89
Petipa, Marius, 135
Petrushka, 50, 101
Picasso, Pablo, 77
Pickford, Mary, 38
Pierrot, 67, 76, 77, 79, 96, 99, 100, 104, 138, 175
Pierrot, 77
Pillar of Fire, 113, 140, 142
Plays and Players in Modern Italy (McLeod), 168
Poetics (Aristotle), 44
Poland, 173
Polite World, The (Brinson and Wildeblood), 168
Popov, Oleg, 83, 173
Prévost, Françoise, 72, 74
Prince Igor, 50
Principles of Dance and Drama (Bharata Muni), 52

Prodigal Son, 111, 140
Prokofiev, Serge, 143
Proteus, 50
Psychedelic, 173
Punchinello, 65
Pylades of Cilicia, 49

Rake's Progress, The, 110, 140, 142
Rāmāyana, 60, 61, 63, 64, 125, 135
Rambert, Ballet, 108
Raymonda, 170
Reinhardt, Max, 104
Religious orders and gesture, 55, 56, 164
Rich, John, 74, 121, 172
Rimsky-Korsakov, 92
Roman Stage, The (Beare), 47
Romantic ballet, 87, 89
Rome, 46, 47, 48, 49, 50, 51, 56, 64, 65, 67, 120, 121, 136
Romeo and Juliet (MacMillan), 27, 35, 36, 89, 110, 140, 142, 143, 144, 146, 155
Romeo and Juliet (Shakespeare), 168
Romeo and Juliet (Tudor), 113
Royal Ballet, 27, 89, 99, 108, 147, 149
Royal Danish Ballet, 87
Runanine, Borislav, 149
Russia, 83, 90, 91, 173

Sadler's Wells Ballet, 92
Sadler's Wells Theatre, London, 79
Sakharoffs, 110
Sallé, Marie, 72, 74
Samosata, 49
Schéhérezade, 50
Senegal Ballet, 116
Seven Deadly Sins, 106
Severin, 100
Shakespeare, 58, 68, 69, 71, 142, 144, 175
Shawn, Ted, 93, 113, 168
Shearer, Moira, 92
Sheik, The, 38
Shepard, Lionel, 115

Index

Sicily, 46, 49, 67
Simon, 91
Sindiely, 116
Sleeping Beauty, The, 13, 90, 135, 147, 155
Song of Victorious Love, The, 91
Sophron of Syracuse, 49
Soul Kiss, The, 96
Spain, 49, 153
St. Denis, Ruth, 93, 110, 113
St. Paul, 48
Stanislavsky, Konstantin, 104
Strange Dream of a Clown, A. See Fools, The
Swan Lake, 12, 13, 17, 24, 25, 61, 135, 155
Switzer, Mary, 166
Sylphide, La, 149
Sylphides, Les, 101
Syracuse, 49

Tales of Hoffmann, The, 92
Tarentule, La, 89
Tati, Jacques, 106, 172
Tavern Bilkers, The, 75
Tchaikovsky, Peter Ilich, 140
Tcherina, Ludmilla, 92
Thailand, 65, 124, 125, 129, 130
Theater of Jean-Louis Barrault (Barrault), 170
Théâtre de Mime Français, 104
Theater on the Balustrade, Prague, 175
Theodora, Empress, 51
Three-Cornered Hat, The, 102
Thunderball, 163
Tibet, 65
Ticktack code, 162, 163
Times, London, 89
Tommazewski, 173

Traffic direction, 162
Tristan and Isolde, 58
Tsuchigumo, 60
Tudor, Antony, 110, 113, 140

Ulanova, Galina, 156
Underwater swimming, 163
United States, 83, 93, 110, 111, 113, 115, 166
United States Vocational Rehabilitation Administration, 166
USSR. *See* Russia

Vieux-Colombier, Théâtre de, Paris, 104
Vigano, Salvatore, 76, 90
Von Laban, Rudolf, 37, 93, 108
Von Swaine, Alexander, 110

Wague, Georges, 100
Waley, Arthur, 134
Walkabout (Chauvel), 44
Weaver, John, 74, 75
Webster, John, 71, 72
Weidman, Charles, 111, 175
Where Three Roads Meet, 87
Whisperers, The, 157
White Devil, The, 71
Wigman, Mary, 93, 108
Wildeblood, Joan, 168
Williams, Dudley, 116
Wormser, 96
Wroclaw Pantomime Theater, 173

Youth, Maturity, Old Age and Death, 172

Zanfretta, Francesca, 96, 99
Zucchi, Virginia, 90